KT-513-047

025564
25564
ACCESSION NUMBER

How to turn round a company

DAVID DAVIS

How to turn round a company

A practical guide to company rescue

■ ■ ■

Published in association with the Institute of Directors

DIRECTOR BOOKS

Published by Director Books,
Fitzwilliam Publishing Limited,
Simon & Schuster International Group,
Fitzwilliam House, 32 Trumpington Street,
Cambridge CB2 1QY, England

First published 1988

British Library Cataloguing in Publication Data
Davis, David
How to turn round a company.
A practical guide to Company rescue.
1. Great Britain. Companies. Mergers & take-overs. Management aspects
I. Title II. Institute of Directors
658.1'6'0941

ISBN 1-870555-02-3

Designed by Geoff Green
Typeset by Hands Fotoset, Leicester
Printed in Great Britain by A. Wheaton and Co. Ltd, Exeter

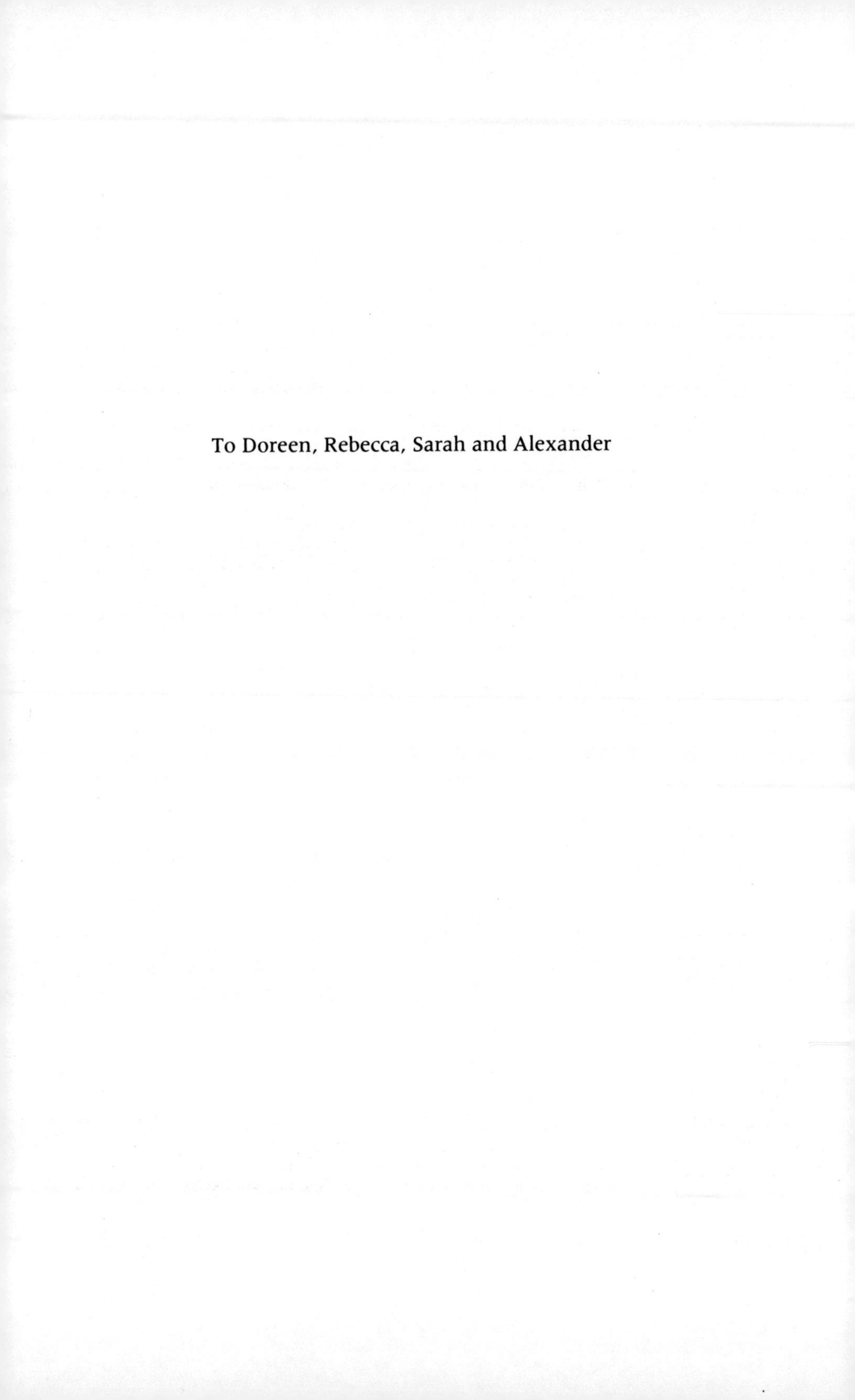

To Doreen, Rebecca, Sarah and Alexander

Contents

Acknowledgements

■

Any book of this nature builds upon the experience of many people. I would like to express my thanks, therefore, to those from whom I learned many of the lessons described herein.

My company, Tate & Lyle plc, has been one of the turnaround success stories of the last decade. The architects of that success, Lord Jellicoe, Sir Robert Haslam and Neil Shaw, provided a host of information on 'how to do it' as well as giving me a chance to try my own ideas, for both of which I am grateful.

From time to time I have been lucky enough to cross the paths of people who were brilliant practitioners in some of the areas I have described. Among these the most salient have been, Jim Scott, who was possibly the best leader I have ever met; Frank Thomlinson, who was the master of devising straightforward strategies from the most complex of systems; and John Mitchell, who was superb at translating difficult strategies into operational reality in the harshest of environments. Outside the company I have been fortunate enough to know, and learn from, one of the greatest articulators of good leadership in post-war Britain, John Garnett.

I also express my gratitude to all of the unsung heroes who worked with me and for me in some of the most difficult days. Without them and their commitment and their ingenuity any amount of managerial skill and inspired leadership is wasted. Most recent among them is Fiona Barron, who typed the drafts for this book, and showed enormous tolerance and patience in doing so.

In addition, this book builds upon the work both of leading academics and practitioners in this field. The most important of these are Bibeault, Argenti and Slatter, who between them virtually created this area of study. Although I have disagreed with them from time to time in this book there is no doubt that they have created the foundations of success upon which any manager can reasonably rely. In addition, there are the authors in the avant-garde of modern business thinking, including Michael Porter, Tom Peters, Robert Heller, Walter Goldsmith, David Clutterbuck, Donald Clifford and Robert Cavanagh, all of whom have added materially to the understanding of business and management in the last decade. Like so many of my fellow practitioners I have gained enormously from the light of understanding they have cast on the most complex of tasks.

Finally, may I thank those people at Harvard who in their teaching have helped to crystallise some of my thoughts in this area. There are many who have contributed to this process but foremost among them must be Bob Glauber, Earl Sasser, Warren Macfarlane and George Lodge. Rarely can a student of such little talent have gained so much from so many in such a short time.

David Davis

Introduction

■

This book is aimed principally at the practitioners of company rescue. It is for those people who lead or wish to lead such rescues, those who choose and select these leaders, and those who invest in the companies that need such rescue. It will also, I hope, be of interest to those who work in such companies.

Quite definitely this book is not an academic treatise. It is not designed as such, and probably there are more comprehensive books that give a full compass of the theories about how one takes on company rescue and that provide the body of supporting references. The reason for the way this book is presented is that turnaround specialists have to be many things: they have to be smart, they have to be tough, but above all they have to be quick. They are notably overburdened with information to absorb and documents to read. Their time is inevitably in short supply. Since this book is principally for the practitioners, it is aimed at being economical with time while not being too economical with truth. Accordingly it does not go into very detailed analyses of individual industries or of individual countries, although these can influence the likely success of the rescue attempt.

To facilitate its use this book is organised in three sections, namely evaluation of the company (Chapters 1, 2 and 3), planning the rescue (Chapters 4, 5, 6 and 7), and phases of the rescue (Chapters 8, 9 and 10). To a limited extent each section is free standing and can be read separately. Furthermore, each section may be of differing interest to the various audiences for this book. For example, the evaluation section is essentially analytical and will be of particular interest to investors in companies in trouble, whereas the planning section might well be of interest to anybody taking over an organisation from scratch, though it is of course critical to the key person in the turnaround, namely the new chief executive. Finally, the phases-of-rescue section is intended only to give the flavour of each phase. The main importance of this section is that it describes transition to the end result for which we are aiming, namely a thriving company with good prospects. The drawback of this structure is that a small degree of repetition occurs in some chapters.

Clearly this book is aimed at companies in need of rescue. However, many of the techniques described within these pages can equally be applied to mediocre or underperforming companies in the aftermath of a takeover. Although such application will lack some of the sense of crisis that is a necessary part of several of the methods described, broadly the methods still work. Nevertheless, the principal interest of this book is with rescue of companies that are making losses and, generally associated with this, those companies that have negative cash flows.

The turnaround expert who is sent in to rescue an ailing company is often portrayed in the literature as a hero. Certainly in the aftermath of a rescue it may look that way; but when he enters the company this is rarely the case. He will probably face vested interests that have for too long remained unchallenged and whose influence he will have to break as part of the recovery strategy. In addition, a number of other stresses will act upon him. There will be time pressures, created by the clamour of customers, creditors, investors and employees. He may have to move to forestall the defensive actions by any of these groups, and indeed to pre-empt aggressive actions taken by his competitors. He will work in an environment of tension created by the physical and emotional pressures of threats to jobs and threatened losses to all the stakeholders in the company. In due course he will also face those pressures himself.

In the midst of this maelstrom of organisational and emotional pressures the turnaround specialist will have two things going for him. Firstly, it will be very apparent, or he will be able to make it apparent, that without radical action on his part all will be lost for the organisation. The prospects of such loss for suppliers, customers, employees and investors will give him an unparalled negotiating leverage. Secondly, precisely because he is new and has no association with the disasters that made the rescue attempt necessary, he will have a 'honeymoon period' in which he can achieve more than is normal in most organisations.

Both advantages are extremely perishable. They are unlikely to last more than a year and will probably last 100 days. Since he must use these advantages to launch the rescue, the turnaround specialist has to move very quickly indeed. Most importantly, the new chief executive's priorities are these:

1. To establish whether or not the business has any long-term viability.
2. If the business can be made viable, to determine the broad routes of survival both immediate and long term. If they cannot be made viable, to determine the most profitable or least-cost escape route for the current owners.
3. To set up the negotiating position for strategies to maximise the probability of success of survival or the exit strategy decided upon.

All these must be done before any significant implementation is started. Accordingly, in ideal circumstances they should be completed before the chief executive arrives on site at the problem company headquarters. Although not always possible, it is often surprising how much can be gleaned about a company's problem from consultants' reports, financial figures, newspaper and magazine articles, reporting on competitors and indeed attitudes of customers. If the company is a subsidiary, then generally massive amounts of data are available although often in four or five different places within the organisation (e.g. central accounting, personnel, research and development, technical services, or planning departments). Very often the simple act of compiling the data from these separate sources will give an enormous previously unseen insight into the problems the company suffers.

The first step, therefore, is to detect the failure and then to analyse its causes. Logically, the process is easy to understand when approached in reverse, namely by first analysing the causes, and that is how this will be dealt with in this book.

CHAPTER 1

Causes of decline

■

It is sometimes helpful to analyse causes of decline in two different ways, namely internal versus external and one-off versus continuous. This is demonstrated in Table 1.1, with some examples written into the boxes.

Table 1.1. Examples of causes of decline

	Internal	External
One-off	Major project failure Poor diversification	Commodity price shock Political intervention
Continuous	Poor control systems Cost slippage	Major technology change Low-cost foreign competition

From Table 1.1 it is evident that a major project failure is essentially an internally inspired problem, but one that is one-off in its impact. At the other extreme the onset of a major change in production technology and the onset of low-price foreign competition are both external problems that are continuous in their effect. This analysis, although rather simplistic, can be helpful in assessing both the effort required and the difficulty of achieving success. Size and longevity of management effort to solve the problem increase as one moves down the table, and difficulty of solving the problem (or probability of failure) increases as one moves from left to right. Thus coping with major changes in product technology and with the low labour costs and high productivity of modern foreign competiton are both extremely difficult and represent high levels of managerial effort over the very long term.

Table 1.1 presents only a static representation. Quite often companies will occupy the bottom left-hand corner of the table, but it will not affect their profits until they come under the cold blast of external competitive pressures. It is therefore quite possible to have a problem which brackets two quadrants of this table. Furthermore, the divisions between the boxes are extremely grey, as evidently some of the problems itemised are at the border lines.

To put this another way, most companies generally fail because they do not respond to external changes. Sometimes this is because they cannot, but more often the reason is complacency, incompetence, or both. Competiton always hits hardest at companies that have not been monitoring their external environment. Examples of companies that die because of an inescapable external effect make up less than one in five of all company bankruptcies, possibly one in ten. The clearly escapable problems make up between a quarter and a half of corporate demises, leaving the remainder in the grey area between the internal and the external.

Internal causes

MANAGEMENT

At the outset it should be stated that a number of the characteristics of management that cause terminal decline in many companies are virtually indistinguishable from those that are responsible for success in a large number of new companies. Occasionally the very same managers who created the company's success will neatly see the company into its grave. It is *inappropriate* management that kills companies. What constitutes appropriate management changes significantly during the life cycle of a company, most especially when it comes under competitive threat.

ONE-MAN RULE

Most writers on company decline (such as Stuart Slatter and Donald Bibeault) come to the conclusion that one-man rule is the cause of much management decline.[1,2] This is not surprising since most of our companies have one chief executive who bears the responsibility for the success or failure of the company. An alternative analysis would show that various types of failure occur under one-man rule. The sections that follow indicate just some of the principal causes of 'failure by dictatorship'.

Complacency

The problem of sleepy management, headed by a complacent chief executive, is common in long-standing firms in very stable industries, particularly where the management has been in place for a very long time. The classical symptoms are unawareness of actual or potential new competiton, insensitivity to customer interests, absence of long-term cost improvements or quality improvements to the products, and slow response times to external changes. Complacency also occasionally occurs with companies that have been widely feted as successful and have begun to believe their own propaganda. The extent to which companies suffer such a management problem depends upon the fundamentals of the competition in the market place. As a rough rule of thumb so long as the company has not been in this complacent framework for too long, the company is recoverable.

Panic paralysis

The opposite of complacency, although it may follow on from it, panic paralysis occurs when the company gets into so much trouble that the chief executive is overwhelmed and becomes incapable of making a decision. Rarely caused by the personality of the chief executive, this is much more frequently the result of the onslaught of a number of problems simultaneously. As a rough rule of thumb, highly successful companies have one strategic problem to deal with, normal companies have two, and problem companies have three or more. The judgement that has to be made is 'how many major strategic problems are there, can they be treated independently, and can they be solved simultaneously?'

Incompetent mangement

Company chief executives are rarely stupid. Businesses are not run successfully on pure intellect, however. Indeed, modern studies indicate that successful management is much less of a clear-cut analytical process than used to be believed.[3] Often the nominally analytical decisions are taken by long-established rules of thumb that can be tested only by long experience in the industry. Information assimilation is often achieved only by many informal contacts, and it is developed over many years in the industry. It is therefore perfectly possible for highly intelligent people to make very bad decisions, particularly if they are in an industry new to them. This is likely to be doubly the case if they have moved from a low-margin, high-volume commodity industry to a high-margin, low-volume product-differentiated industry, or vice versa. If such is the principal problem, then the business tends to have a very high probability of recovery, so long as the 'incompetent' chief executive has not driven away all of the second-tier high-quality management.

A prisoner of history

Companies are, quite reasonably, likely to stick with their successes. Unfortunately, over time all successes eventually become obsolete whether they are products or business strategies. The result is that companies following such strategies become prisoners of history. This is a common problem when the chief executive has been very long serving, often being the creator of the company itself. It can also happen to his successors, however. The fact is that general rules are passed on from one generation to another. Gordon Donaldson and Jay Lorsch report the following case, as described to them:

> A consumer products . . . spoke about what he had learned from one of his older superiors:
> 'He gave me three pieces of advice when I was working for him in Europe:
>
> 1. You'd better not be short of product. You're better off having too much inventory at times.
> 2. Don't touch anything, but [brand name] – a piece of advice I now don't believe in.
> 3. Don't let your price get lower than [a major competitor]. We sell for less in the States, and our image is lower, but in Europe we are equals.
>
> We got along fine as long as I followed those rules. He made sure I got whatever support I needed.'
>
> In other words, as long as he stayed within existing principles he took no flak. For competitive younger executives who are committed to advancing in their company, such treatment would be an important lesson in continuing advancement. Clearly an experience like this provides a powerful incentive to learn and to accept such beliefs. Further, it is likely that the selection and hiring of young managers facilitates this acceptance of beliefs. The newcomer may be chosen, and may choose to join the company, because his personality is compatible with the beliefs of those doing the hiring. Thus the new manager joins the firm predisposed to live by its principles.[4]

These rules can be perpetuated in this way until the firm is hit by the onslaught of competition. Then it gets into trouble. The probability of recovery under these circumstances is determined by the extent to which the competition has run ahead of the company and by the resources the company has to catch up.

Other executives

The problem of other executives falls into three categories: quality, skills, and direction.

Quality

The longer a company has been in decline, the poorer its quality of management will be. It is possible to recover a company with poor-quality management, but to do so requires much more effort, is much more difficult, and requires some special techniques, most of which are aimed at ensuring that new management is not crippled by the attitudes and practices of the old.

Skills

A frequent characteristic of failed companies is to have gaps in the skills of the second-tier management. Often this occurs because the company is dominated by one class of people, frequently a reflection of the chief executive himself. For example, many British engineering companies used to be dominated by engineers. Irrespective of what the skill is, management is one area where uniformity is dangerous. Any company whose second-tier management does not include at least one leader is each of finance, marketing, and operational or production management is severely at risk. What is frequently also overlooked is that each of these managers should be capable of proper leadership – they should not be 'yes men'. The chief executive must encourage them to debate strategies and tactics, prior to the decision, and they must be able to champion their own aspect of the business, at the same time having sufficient capability to comprehend the strategic impact of other specialist functions in the business as a whole.

Direction

Another characteristic of failed companies is a lack of proper consensus about the strategy of the company. Generally speaking this lack of consensus means that the strategy has not been properly tested in debate and as such is poor in quality and lacks the proper commitment of the key leaders in the organisation. It also means that different departments are probably working in different directions.

These matters ought to be blinding glimpses of the obvious. The problem is that these weaknesses in leadership – for that is what they are – occur quite commonly even in successful companies.

POOR FINANCIAL CONTROL

An organisation's accounts provide the single most consistent, most reliable, and most relevant information available to the majority of managers. Accountancy provides both the scoreboard and the lingua franca of business. The inability to maintain and use the system is not just a failure in its own right; it is an acid test of the management's competence to use information more generally in pursuit of its organisation's goals. It is the failure to seek and use information when the outside world is changing that more than anything else leads to the demise of companies.

The major problems that occur in financial control are as follows:

1. Inability to forecast and control cash flow.
2. Inadequate or non-existent profit and costing systems.
3. No budgetary control.
4. Poor use of those systems that exist.

Individually or collectively, these faults are found in a very high proportion of companies that go bankrupt.

Cash flow

A shortage of cash virtually always precipitates the final bankruptcy of companies in decline. Not surprisingly, therefore, the inability to manage cash is an important cause of failure. The two key tools in a cash management system are the cash flow forecast and the cash control system. The ability to create an effective cash flow forecast itself is a measure of the management's understanding of how its cash flow works. In order to draw up a decent forecast it is necessary to identify the key variables that influence cash movements, to resolve the issues and accountability that relate to these variables, and where appropriate to design policies for the most efficient use of cash. The output of such as forecasting system, namely how much cash will be needed, is both an important management tool and a method of inspiring confidence in creditors and bankers.

Cash control systems, behind all the jargon, essentially just answer the questions 'How much cash do we have? Where is it? Where is it coming from? and What is it being used for?' A good cash control system also indicates the answer to the most important question, 'What can we do about it?' If the management cannot answer these questions, it is not in control of its cash system, and even if it manages everything else well, it still exposes the company to unnecessary risk.

Profit and costing systems

As a fundamental part of a management accounting system, profit and costing systems provide crucial data for both decision-making and incentive systems. A good system will allow a manager to identify the total, average, and marginal costs of production by every significant product and by every location. It should tie in with the physical control systems used in the production, distribution, and sales systems. It should enable managers to know whether their methods are improving on previous years and whether they are achieving their budgets (see the section that follows). And it should enable sales and commercial managers to know the costs of increasing output of any particular product and the margin available to them on such increases. A good profit and costing system is the key to any method of assessing a decision both before and after that decision is taken. In its absence even the brightest manager can do little more than make educated guesses, which is generally a good formula for corporate collapse.

Budgetary control

In the majority of businesses a budgetary control system is a necessity and the absence of it will make competent management impossible. An effective budgetary control system is possible only when it is built on top of a well-designed profit and costing system. Like such a system it must accurately reflect the physical processes that make up the business. It should be built up from numbers of units of output, and all the components of cost and price, be they numbers of sales representatives or numbers of kilowatts of electricity used to produce a given product. Designed in this way, the budget allows a manager to know when a variance arises from sources outside his control, and when it arises from causes inside his control.

Variance analysis itself provides a flagging mechanism that allows managers to allocate their time to solving the most important problems, and as such it is a fundamental component of the company's directional control system. Also, crucially, it allows the manager to draw a link between actions and decisions taken, as well as results on the bottom line.

Poor use

Inadequate use of the systems available is widespread in problem companies. There are many reasons for this, as follows:

Competence

Very often managers have little training in the use of their specific financial and operational control systems. For most managers this modicum of training can still be achieved in one day flat – so ignorance is virtually an inforgivable sin. This poor competence, however, is often compounded by the system itself. Ponderous and incomprehensible systems that take too long to produce and are then too long to absorb will confound even a very good manager. Speed, accuracy and simplicity are necessary features of good financial control systems. All are achievable with the existence of personal computers today.

Decentralisation

The effectiveness of any organisation is directly influenced by how close the decision maker is to the thing he is trying to change. How close the marketing manager is to the market in organisational terms, or how close the production manager or engineering manager is to the production unit also in organisational terms, influences the manager's speed of response and the availability of other information necessary to fill out and back up the accounting data the manager handles. This is what I call D^3, or Data-Decision Distance factor, in design of financial control systems. To minimise this factor, and thereby maximise the manager's effectiveness, the information system should be organised along accountability lines. Again, this is a matter of appropriate information: if the manager is responsible for a profit centre, he should have the profitability information; if he is responsible for gross margin on sales, he should have that data. This apparently self-evident rule is observed more in the breach than in the commission. In failing companies information is often hoarded at the centre.

Accordingly, one of the commonest features of successful turnarounds is that they include a high degree of decentralisation of decision making. Similarly, accounting systems give information to the decentralised units and to the accountable manager.

Hierarchy

The organisational equivalent of decentralisation is forcing the decision making down to the lowest level possible in the organisation. The financial control system should encourage this by feeding appropriate information to the lowest level managers, and by ensuring that the all-important follow-up system operates at this level. None of this will work, however, without proper authority being vested at a low enough level in the organisation.

Practical considerations

It should always be possible to assess the physical action necessary to correct a profit or cost problem. As a result it is always worthwhile having accounting systems that integrate with physical control systems or at least are consistent with them. It is also essential to have action plans that relate the achievements expected during the course of the year to their effect on profits. Follow-up on action plans should be as vigorous as follow-up on profits. Further, as the process of performance review carries on through the year, it should generate new action plans that should also have identifiable profit effects. This is a key matter, all too often absent from failing companies.

This section has concentrated on financial control, or the lack of it. Similar problems apply equally to marketing information systems (such as sales reports, call reports, complaint analyses); to production systems (such as quality analyses, maintenance and downtime reports, delivery performance reports); and to personnel systems. They also apply to the management's response to the outside world, or its failure to respond, in reaction to competitor activity and market and technological changes. These are all very important, and blindness in any area can lead to company failure.

There are many ways, therefore, that poor control can manifest itself through failure to analyse the data properly and/or failure to act upon it. That an information system exists does not necessarily mean a control system exists. One of the few good aspects of this most basic of management errors is that a company with a good information system, but without proper managerial control inputs, provides potentially the opportunity for the fastest and most reliable turnaround category there is.

OPERATIONAL CAUSES

In reality operational causes are generally the outcome of the managerial failures described earlier. However, they may be more recognisable than their own original causes. They are principally high costs and poor marketing (including poor product design).

High costs

High costs can arise for many reasons, some internal, some external, some neither one nor the other (such as poor historical location with respect to, say, labour costs or government policies). The major internal causes are typically outcomes of previous decisions or long-established practice, such as the following:

1. Plant size, with both scale and learning-curve effects on costs.
2. Plant design and product design, and the associated production management practices (including scheduling, planning, maintenance and so forth). These set minima for achievable cost levels and capital employed, and they limit or enhance flexibility.
3. Labour management practices, with the implications for wage costs (and wage oncosts), productivity and flexibility.
4. Administrative decisions, namely the level of company overhead, and provision of central research and development, technical functions, and financial control, can increase central costs but may or may not enhance operational effectiveness by a greater amount.

Alternatively, the high costs may just be a function of poor control systems as outlined earlier.

Poor marketing

Other than by the results, namely declining share and/or margins, poor marketing is much more difficult to assess. Nevertheless, in practice recognising the symptoms of poor marketing is quite easy. Typically the symptoms include one or all of the following:

1. Poor market responsiveness, *either* because of poor information *or* lack of interest in the market, or both. (This often happens in technically driven or financially driven companies).
2. Lack of any innovative response to market demands (low rate of new products and/or product enhancements).
3. Inability to analyse the market and organise a strategy based on a clear understanding of company position as a cost leader, a differentiated supplier, or a focused supplier.

4. No action orientation in marketing or, possibly, an expensive and ineffective one.

ONE-OFF CAUSES

The most significant categories of one-off causes of company failure are catastrophic capital projects and unwise diversification.

Catastrophic capital project

Capital projects that are catastrophic fit certain clear-cut criteria, as follows:

1. They are large in relation to the company, generally unwisely so. Accordingly, their impact both on company profitability and on its cash flow are large enough to overwhelm the inherent profitability of the business. Pay attention to the ratio of project capital cost to assets (worry if it is above 25%) and the proportion of current profits that might be swallowed by project interest costs.
2. They frequently involve new technologies. This can mean technologies that are at the forefront of human knowledge or equally technologies that are merely new to that particular company. In either case there is in the company little skill or previous experience of building such factories or manufacturing operations. As a rough rule of thumb such projects end up costing double or more than double what they were assessed to cost at the feasibility stage. This high capital cost is often matched by high running costs and/or lower output than planned at project approval. Typically with such projects, approval at board level was given when the project was only at its feasibility stage. The wise rule should be to give final approval to such projects only when they are fully engineered and when legally binding contract quotes have been drawn up. Very few companies, however, are sufficiently rigorous to apply this rule.
3. They may involve entering an entirely new market for the company. Normally this is marked by the project achieving very poor sales volumes, way below breakeven level, and often poor margins as well, as a result of competitive response.
4. There is also a category of legitimate hard-luck stories, or strategic decisions that have gone wrong. This can include major strikes, which delay the project; material shifts in world markets or exchange rates during the period when the project is being

completed; withdrawal of approvals for new products; and any number of other commercial tragedies. What is surprising is how often more than one problem hits such projects (so perhaps it is not really bad luck after all?). So long as the core business of a company is viable, something can be rescued from these businesses; but it is not always a particularly profitable outcome for the holders of the company equity. Much of the strategy in such a circumstance is devoted to renegotiating terms with the lenders and investors in the project, often followed by a sale of the project factory, typically to a competitor. Sometimes the rescue attempt will involve making a go of the new project, but the financial cost will increase the vulnerability of the whole business.

Unwise diversification

Unwise diversification is extremely common, but it does not often jeopardise the entire company. Rather like a catastrophic project, the strategy and tactics typically tend to revolve around a minimum-loss disposal strategy; although ironically if the acquired company has a sharp reduction in performance, this can occasionally be turned into an advantageous recovery. This may then be more profitable than a disposal strategy.

The key issue in unwise diversification is that companies are venturing outside their areas of skill and cannot bring anything useful to the management of the acquired company. Accordingly, a rescue expert in this circumstance often has to find new management or revitalise the old management. In doing so he frequently has to prevent corporate headquarters from intervening in the operation of the company. This must be negotiated at the beginning, and he must explicitly exclude intervention when the first thing goes wrong (as it will).

External causes

The two major external causes of decline are competition and market decline. Of course, these two causes are heavily intertwined: significant changes in market demand almost invariably cause radical changes in competitive behaviour; on the other hand, overall market demand is often markedly influenced by the sum of competitive behaviour within the industry (as in the enormous growth of the electronics and computing industries on the back of radical reductions in the costs and prices in those industries).

COMPETITION

Gradual competitor ascendancy is generally a symptom of an internal fault in the company, such as weak cost control or poor marketing management. Competitor activity can strictly be considered an external cause of decline only where there is a marked change or increase in competitive activity over a period of less than five years. This can be brought about either by the entry of a new competitor or by a significant change in the strategy of an old competitor. It should be borne in mind that this is not an unusual occurrence in the environment of most normal (non-failing) companies. There is in a ten-year period anywhere between a one-in-five and a one-in-three chance of a new competitor entering a given market. The higher the growth rate and the higher the profitability of the market, the higher the probability of a new competitor entering.

All the difficult problems arise when that new competitor has a clear external competitive advantage, particularly if that advantage is sustainable. Table 1.2 illustrates this, although it is by no means exhaustive. The table focuses competitive strategy either on price advantage or on product/service advantage versus two of the commonest sources of advantage, namely new technology and lower input costs.

Table 1.2. Strategic focus of competition

	Sources of advantage	
Focus	Technology	Input costs
Price advantage	Better and/or cheaper process	Lower cost bases such as cheap labour and raw material access → volume strategy
Product/service advantage	Product enhancement	Higher profits → greater investment in product development or lower prices

Although most cases of increased competition fit into one of these boxes, there is nothing to say that a new competitor should not fill all of them. Indeed, a number of Japanese industries, enjoying lower labour costs and higher technology held this position in their onslaught on Western industry in the last twenty years. While such an onslaught is not irresistible, it does represent one of the toughest challenges one is likely to face.

In the case both of a new entrant and that of the old competitor with a new-found or newly exploited competitive edge, the aggressive attack on the company's market place generally implies a new productive capacity entering the industry. Price reductions are a sign of this aggression. It should be noted that in Slatter's study of the causes of decline, 20% of the companies that recovered faced price warfare while of those that did not recover, 100% faced it.[5] Under these circumstances the survival chances of a company depend upon the intentions of the new competitor, the size of its spare capacity, its financial capabilities, and whether or not the failing company has the resources and the skills to mimic or improve on the technological and cost advantages held by its opposition.

Product erosion of the company's position – on the basis of improved product quality, better features, or completely new competitors' products – tends to be more symptomatic of the actual day-to-day incremental expansion that most businesses attempt with more or less success. Accordingly, there are more survivors in the face of such an attack. As a general statement this is an overstark comparison; but the main point is that in order to survive, the company has to meet the competition directly or indirectly, or failing that, retreat to a sector of the market that it can defend, and cut its financial and organisational capacity accordingly.

MARKET DECLINE

Market decline falls into two categories, cyclical and secular.

Cyclical decline

It is with some reservation that I classify cyclical decline as an external cause of failure at all, since it causes failure only when the companies concerned either have inadequate resources to cope with the downturns in their industry or fail to make proper adjustments in their cost base and capacity at times of downturn. Both problems could be laid at the door of poor management and poor planning. However, cyclical declines are of variable depth and so arguably they are an external impact. When they are of greater than normal size, they frequently precipitate competitive wars of the type described earlier.

Secular decline

Long-term declines can be demographic, or they can be caused by substitution, by changes in pattern of demand, or for a variety of other reasons. Again, they are marked by price wars and other outbreaks of fierce competition. The principal question for a company in these circumstances is whether or not it is going to be a survivor. This involves judging if and when the secular decline is going to reach a plateau, how the competition is going to cope with it and how much cost reduction and/or niche market defence a company can manage. It is also a circumstance in which bluff is very important (along with the ability to withstand financial pain), since there are frequent periods of temporary over-capacity that are resolved only when one other player in the industry accepts that he will have to close capacity. The strategy under such circumstances resembles a high-stakes game of poker. It can, however, represent a sizeable opportunity inasmuch as cheap capacity is frequently available. Indeed, it is perfectly possible to go from being a small competitor harvesting a declining market to being the largest survivor, given properly executed opportunistic strategies. This is also true, to a lesser extent, in heavily cyclical markets.

ONE-OFF OR CATASTROPHIC

Besides competition and general market trends, one-off or catastrophic events can bring about a company's decline. One-off or catastrophic decline can occur with sharp changes in price structure principally of the main raw material the company uses. The great oil shock of 1973–4 was one classical case, but major movements in commodity prices then and subsequently have created many examples of this problem. Such decline can also apply to property and financial institutions (with interest rates), and on a wider scale to whole economies, if they suffer from hyper-inflation. This category can also include the effects of major political impact, particularly in third world countries, for example, civil wars, shortage of foreign currency or state sequestration of raw material sources.

The principal issues in such circumstances are as follows:

1. Have we the financial resources to withstand the shock?
2. Do we have the negotiation leverage to mitigate the shock?
3. Does this represent a marked change in our competitive position, and is it permanent?

4. Will it have a significant impact on our final market, and can we cope with it?

It should be stressed, however, that there is a great need for honesty in assessing one's own competitive position. It is often very difficult to accept that second best is both what one is and that this is a tenable strategic position.

CHAPTER 2

Symptoms of decline

■

There are two important perspectives from which one must be able to detect decline of companies and, therefore, the need for rescue: from outside the company and from inside, say, a holding company looking at a subsidiary. The other possible perspective, that from inside a declining company, is of less importance because those below the level of chief executive will not have the power to carry out the necessary changes.

If the chief executive himself is reading this book, he has probably already realised the answer to the question posed by this chapter. This point is made because both significant perspectives suffer from one drawback, namely that the information easily available to them is relatively sparse. It is by no means non-existent, but it takes some work to gather and the effort that goes into data gathering may not be economic.

External analysis

Obviously all the 'external' analyses can be applied internally to a company as well as externally. The external approaches have to work on the least possible information. There are two types of external analysis, qualitative and quantitative. The qualitative analysis forecasts the possibility or probability of decline, while the quantitative analysis measures actual decline and extrapolates this to estimate the probability of failure.

QUALITATIVE ANALYSIS

All that qualitative measures do is recognise the major changes to which management is unable or unwilling to respond. The first element of this process is to recognise those major changes that may jeopardise the company's future. The major changes that might adversely influence the fate of a company are covered in some detail in the previous chapter, but those that might be more visible to external observers are the following:

1. Major decline in market size or sharp reduction in growth rate.
2. Major change in market structure.
3. Major change in technology.
4. Major change in competitors (new entrants or a takeover of old competition).
5. Competitive action.

Any of the above changes in what was previously a very stable market place represents a threat to the continued profitable existence of the company. Ironically, it is sometimes the best-run companies in such stable market-places that are the worst hit by these changes. This is because the management of such companies find it hardest to abandon exactly those skills and rules of thumb that have been most successful for so many years. And this is the key to a threatening change becoming a terminal one. A change in the competitive environment can be threatening; but an inappropriate management response can render it terminal.

These changes are the most easily visible steady-state problems that are the most difficult to deal with in company turnarounds. Yet also one-off issues can cripple companies, such as the overlarge project that overruns on cost. Generally speaking, catastrophies are easier to spot and easier to deal with than steady-state problems. They can vary from those involving the renegotiation of a contract (e.g. the RB211 at Rolls Royce) to those which completely destroy the basis of an industry (e.g. the product liability suits that afflicted asbestos producers). The solutions may be either simple or simply impossible.

QUANTITATIVE ANALYSIS

Market indicators

Observers external to a company are restricted to very limited data, mostly that published in the financial accounts. One piece of data that is more telling than any other but is not often available, and takes a great deal of work to obtain when it is, is market share. Persistent declines in market share are the clearest indicators of ill health in a company. Sometimes decline is deliberate and will be associated with enhanced short-term profits. Sacrificing market share for profitability is a legitimate policy when applied to cash generators, but it is obviously one of limited life. It reflects an acceptance that a liquidation of the company is the most profitable outcome for the owners.

The other scenario, that of declining market share with constant or reducing profitability, if a persistent feature of a company's behaviour, is a characteristic of terminal decline. Occasionally market share is held constant, but price competition severely erodes margins. This may be a good managerial response, so long as it is supported by cost reduction/ value enhancement programmes as well.

The other market problem that can be terminal is the long-run secular decline in volumes of the whole market place. Invariably such decline spells trouble, and may be impossible to survive.

Financial measures

Measures that rely on accounting figures are subject to the vagaries of accounting practice. Outside Britain and the United States and countries of similar standards, such as Canada, accounting practice is often dominated by the need to conceal rather than the intent to disclose. All that follows, therefore, assumes the sort of enlightened accounting practice followed by British, US and similar accounting professions.

Even so, managers never like to admit to problems, and one of the characteristics of failing companies is the attempt to conceal them. Thus changes in treatment of depreciation, research and development, asset valuations, pensions and other deferred provisions are all warning signs to look deeper into a company's health. Similarly, delayed accounts, accounts qualified by auditors, and indeed changes of auditors, whilst not necessarily sufficient reasons to base adverse judgements upon, are certainly reasons for closer inspection. Nevertheless, despite attempts to conceal problems, it is possible to determine a great deal from the profit and loss accounts and balance sheet of any given company.

The first test of a company's health is obviously its profitability. This is the measure of how much a company is adding to society, the measure of how much the value of what it makes exceeds the value of what is uses. The only drawback of this measure is that it is easier to bias by dubious accounting techniques than are other less judgemental measures, such as cash flow. The other message of this section is, then, 'read the small print' – in this case review the company's accounting policies and judge whether the policy is a proper reflection of reality.

Once a company is insufficiently profitable, which occurs when its return on capital falls below its cost of capital, the next question that must be applied is, 'how long has it got?' Virtually all companies that die essentially bleed to death in financial terms. Financial tests are, therefore, 'how fast are we bleeding?' and 'how much blood do we have left?' The rate of bleeding is the size of the negative cash flow. Once that is determined, we need to know the level of resources available and then we can calculate the expected life of the company. On a very rough-and-ready basis, the resources available are just the total assets less the total debts or, put another way, the sum of the equity and accumulated reserves. In reality, of course, the assets are often worth less than their value on the books. We might add in the sophistication of the company's ability to raise new money, which if still nominally profitable the company may be able to do.

Z-score analysis

Two or three methods of assessing this process have been developed. The first – Z-score analysis – was pioneered in the United States by Altman.[6] It was then taken up in the United Kingdom by Taffler and Tisshaw and Argenti.[7,8] The Z-score was not devised analytically but arrived at by a statistical technique, discriminant analysis. Nevertheless, as Altman's formula demonstrates, it essentially measures in a number of ways the ratios of rate of loss of cash to resources available.[9]

Altman's formula was calculated for US companies as follows:

$$Z = 1.2X_1 + 1.4X_2 + 3.3X_3 + 0.6X_4 + X_5$$

X_1 = working capital/total assets
X_2 = retained profits/total assets
X_3 = profit before interest and tax/total assets
X_4 = (market value of equity plus preference shares)/total liabilities
X_5 = sales/total assets

The large commercial company Datastream applies a variant of this technique to a large number of companies in the United Kingdom. Figure 2.1 shows the average Z-score of the group of failed firms against that of the population of non-failed firms in the years before failure. As can be seen, the Z-score shows both a significant absolute difference and a marked downward trend for the firms that failed.

For individual companies the measure is not quite so clear cut. The distribution of Z-scores for the failed and the non-failed companies shows some degree of overlap, the more so the earlier the measure is assessed, as can be seen in Fig. 2.2 and Fig. 2.3. This is to be expected;

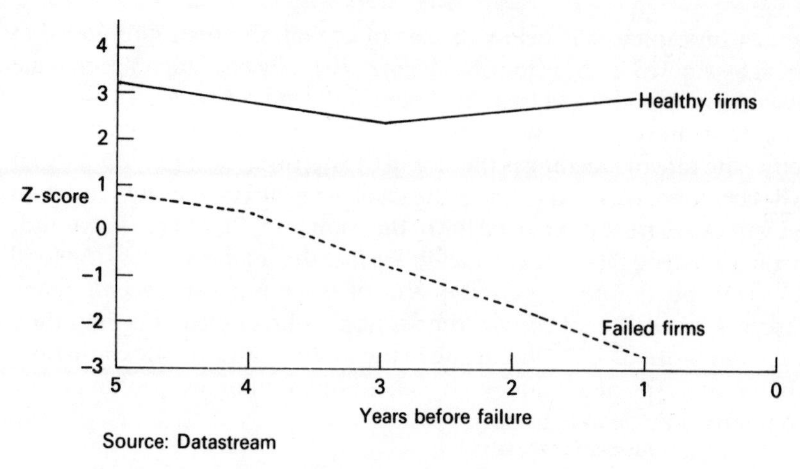

Fig. 2.1. Trends in average values for the years prior to failure.

partly because any measurement system has inaccuracies, but mostly because the management of the companies at risk presumably struggle to recover, in some cases successfully.

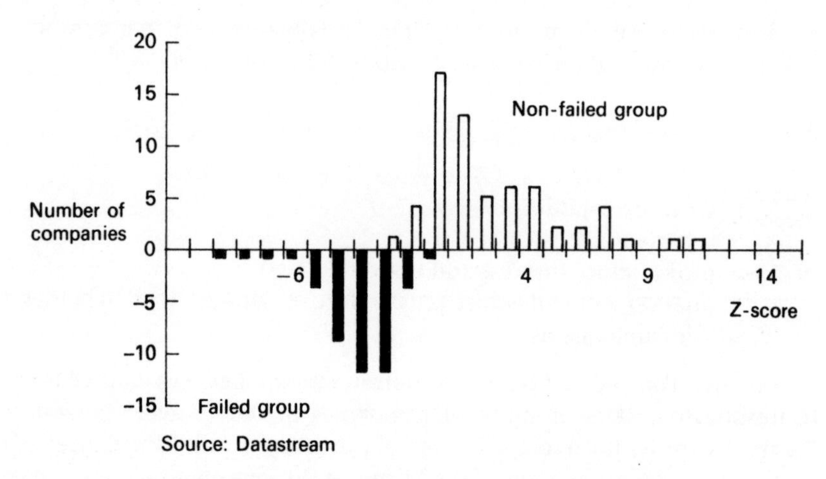

Fig. 2.2. Distribution of Z-scores one year before failure.

The accuracy of the Z-score classification as calculated on the Datastream basis is highlighted in Table 2.1 and compared with cruder tests of solvency. One year before failure, one failed (2%) and six non-failed (10%) firms were misclassified.

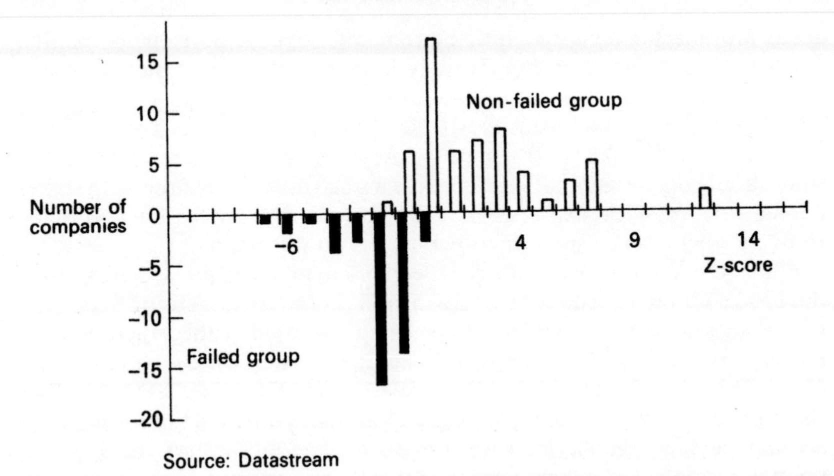

Fig. 2.3. Distribution of Z-scores two years before failure.

Table 2.1. Number of failed (F) and non-failed (NF) firms misclassified

	Number of firms misclassified					
	One year before failure		Two years before failure		Three years before failure	
	F	NF	F	NF	F	NF
Current ratio	4	24	7	25	6	30
Quick ratio	3	15	6	21	10	20
Z-score model	1	6	4	7	12	10
No. observations	46	60	46	60	44	60

Source: Datastream.

Perhaps the best description of the use of Z-scores is given by Datastream itself:

Clearly, some comment on the interpretation of Z-scores is called for. The Z-score has typically been used as an index of financial vulnerability, but this figure should be interpreted with the utmost caution, and certainly never used in isolation. A low Z-score does not imply that a firm will fail, merely that it is exhibiting characteristics similar to those of past failures. Consequently no decision as to the future viability of the firm can be taken without a further analysis. It should be stressed that the Z-score is a complement to further analysis, not a substitute for it, although one of its most effective uses will be to act as a primary filter for identifying companies whose developing financial characteristics demand further, possibly urgent, evaluation. A steady decline would indicate a deteriorating financial position, but even then subsequent failure would be by no means inevitable. Firms are restructured and recover, and others may be taken over while the potential of a firm's shares as a recovery stock should not be ignored. After all, only a small minority of firms with shares quoted on the Stock Exchange actually go into receivership, and so-called recovery stocks can be spectacular performers on the market.

While the Z-score has primarily been used to highlight a deteriorating financial position, it is equally useful as an index of strength. A rising trend in Z-scores suggests that profitability is not being increased at the expense of the longer term viability of the company. In Fig. 2.4, the trend in Z-scores for MFI is contrasted with the trends for Dunbee–Combex–Marx and EMI. MFI has shown a very rapid rise in Z-scores over the last four years, and this rise has been accompanied by a similar increase in market value. By contrast, the declining trend for Dunbee–Combex–Marx and EMI has ended in receivership and takeover respectively.[10]

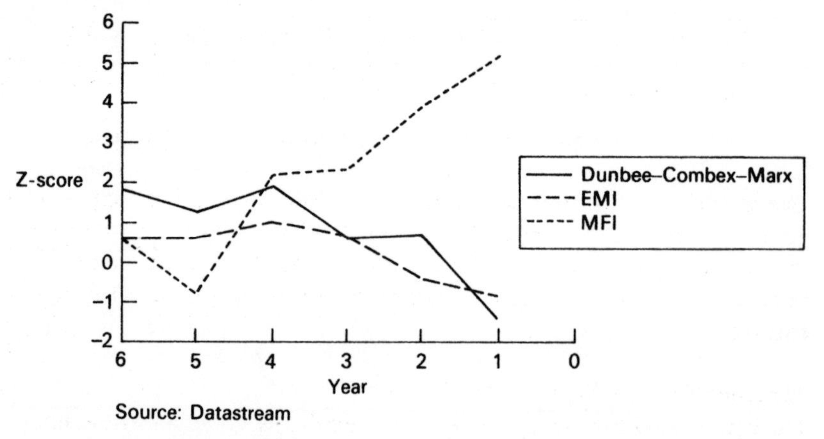

Fig. 2.4. Comparative Z-scores for EMI, MFI and Dunbee–Combex–Marx.

In this case Z-scores effectively fulfilled their function of predicting failure. Used with proper circumspection, they are also useful as measures of overall financial health. Datastream again:

Inter-firm ranking should be interpreted with appropriate caution, because clearly no two companies are identical. Company size is also relevant, as smaller firms are often less able to weather financial storms than larger ones. However, provided that those general reservations are borne in mind, companies may fairly be compared within the same sector. Probably the three most similar companies quoted on the Stock Exchange are the mail order firms Grattan

Warehouses, Empire Stores and Freemans. Whereas Empire has broadly maintained its position in terms of market value and market share, the respective positions of Freemans and Grattan have been reversed in recent years, although the trends which led to this were clearly evident long before that. The trend in Z-scores is illustrated in Fig. 2.5 and their trends closely parallel the fortunes of these three firms.[11]

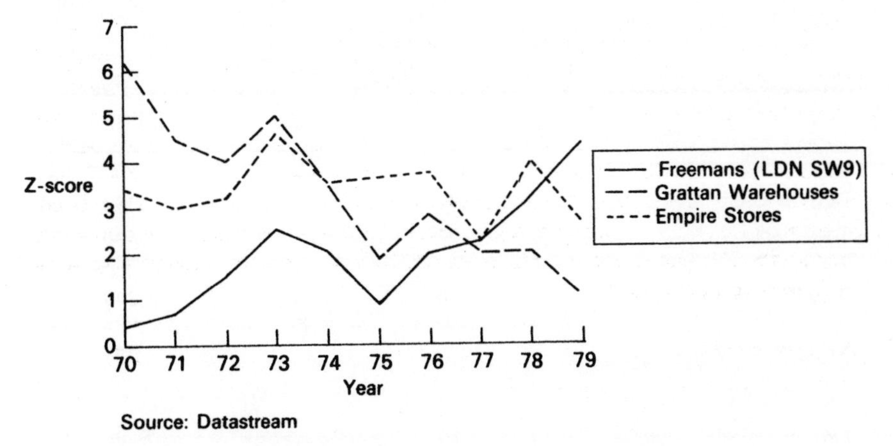

Fig. 2.5. Z-scores for Freemans, Grattan, and Empire Stores.

The lesson to be drawn from this is that while the Z-score technique is good as a measure of risk of failure, it is also not bad as a general thermometer of corporate financial health. It is, therefore, worth bearing in mind as a single-figure measure of company performance throughout a rescue attempt.

The gamblers' ruin method

The other quantitative approach quite explicitly calculates how long a company has left by comparing its use of resources with the resources it has left. This approach to the problem, known as the 'gamblers' ruin', was devised by Jarrod Wilcox. It attempts to value the assets of a company explicitly on a breakup or open market resale basis. To do so, it applies a set of valuation rules to the balance sheet of the company concerned. The specific approach taken by Wilcox assumes that fixed assets on the open market are worth half their value in the books, and that current assets are worth 70% of their value in the books. Using these ratios the method assesses the resources in a company's balance sheet and the extent to which these resources are used up both by negatively operating cash flow and by the loss of value as cash is turned into fixed or current assets. As a predictor of bankruptcy, this model is about 80% accurate, a little less than the Altman Z-score analyses described earlier. This method does, however, have the advantage of being clearly analytical. It is possible to predict easily the impact of financial actions upon this calculation.

Table 2.2. Gamblers' ruin liquidation value
(Values illustrative only, in £000's)

	Book	Ratio	Value
Fixed assets	800	0.5	400
Current assets	200	0.7	140
Total assets	1000		540
Total debt	300	1	300
'Equity'	700	n/a	240
Value invested in Co.	1000		540
Change in value			
Earnings	80		80
Dividends	30	−1	−30
Net capital expenditure	120	−0.5	−60
Additions to current assets	30	−0.3	−9
Change in resources	50		−19

The example in Table 2.2 demonstrates the point. A marginally profitable company has equity of £700,000 and debt of £300,000. The book value of the total assets amounts to £1 million, but its estimated liquidation value amounts only to £540,000. Accordingly, the real value of equity and reserves is only £240,000. Further, the company is expanding its capital base, and the loss of value in converting cash to assets causes the book *increase* in reserves to become a *reduction* in value. The company has significant value left, but were it to go into loss with, perhaps, commitments to complete its capital programme, it would rapidly slide towards a nil net value (or equity) position. On the basis of these numbers, at breakeven it would have five or six years left, unless the capital programme improved its profitability markedly. Cutting capital expenditure might extend this lifespan if it did not *significantly* worsen the earnings position.

Other methods

Finally, there is the much simpler ratio of cash flow to debt. This is of course easier to calculate than any of the other methods. This simpler ratio is not a bad predictor of viability in its own right.[12]

All these measures quantify to a greater or lesser extent the possibility of bankruptcy. The fact of the matter is that they are all measures of how badly a company is bleeding away its vital financial resources against the quantity of those resources that are left.

Internal analysis

Internal measures fall into three categories, strategic, operational, and financial.

STRATEGIC MEASURES

The aim of strategic measures is to give forewarning of major shifts in the competitive arena that will in the long term affect corporate profitability. By their very nature these measures are qualitative rather than quantitative. They may be categorised as changes in competitive position, technological changes, and changes in the strategic negotiating environment.

Competitive position

New entrants, particularly if they are of significant financial power, have a material quantity of capacity to add to the market, have a significant competitive advantage (i.e. cost, quality, product or service advantage) and/or have knowledge of the market place.

Current competitors – major strategic changes in this area include:

1. New capacity, particularly with respect to the size of the market.
2. Integration moves, either backward to capture advantageous raw material positions or forward to capture markets.
3. New ownership, which may change the aggressiveness of the company.

Technology

Adoption of new technology by competition is itself a warning sign. Mostly this change will be easy to monitor, in terms of both the production technology, which will give cost and quality advantages, and also of course product technology, which could give market share advantages. The more difficult area to monitor is that of substitute technology. For companies to stay ahead in this field is effectively impossible, but they can observe threats once they materialise. For example, in the 1960s it was difficult for sugar companies to see the impact of the developments of enzyme technology until that technology allowed high-fructose syrup to create a replacement for sugar in the early 1970s; however they would be able to know when factories to manufacture the product were being built.

Changes in negotiating environment

Strategic changes may undermine a company's negotiating leverage in its markets in terms of both buyers of its product and sellers of its supplies. Significant moves to merger or cartelisation can have a material effect upon the profitability of the company, as has been seen, for example, in the impact of concentration in the UK retail market on sectors of the UK manufacturing industry. Most of all, backward integration by customers and forward integration by suppliers can also represent a significant threat. This was a permanent threat that the American car industry held over its parts suppliers. Finally, competitive pressures that threaten the profitability of the end market can move backward through customers in the form of demands for price cuts from the company. In addition structural changes with any industry can change this negotiating environment. For example, if the capital intensity of the business increases along with others of its competitors as a result of technological changes and perhaps in pursuit of apparent productivity gains, this can easily translate later into the volume-hungry, high breakeven, weak negotiating position of the typical commodity supplier. This is a consequence of capital investment frequently overlooked at the time it is undertaken.

OPERATIONAL MEASURES

Operational measures are general measures of physical variables or market variables. They are all straightforward and described next.

Volume

Either market share decline or decline of the end market can have the effect of reducing volume. Both downturns are early warnings of trouble to come.

Productivity

Productivity applies to capital and to personnel. In capital terms this relates to utilisation and output per pound of capital invested. Productivity should follow a trend of permanent mild increase, even if at only ½% per annum, in all but the oldest industries. Similarly, personnel productivity should show a permanent improvement. Learning effects, new technology, and improved product design can all contribute to upturns. It should be understood that stability is not enough, and very long term stability is probably a warning sign.

Market perception

This is quite difficult to measure, but if available the customers' perception of relative product quality (as a percentage of customers who rate the product above average minus the percentage who rate it below average) is a key variable and if monitored can give very valuable advance indication of the stability of market share. Market share itself, of course, is an indicator of both production and marketing success.

Margin

Margin reflects both price and cost movements. A declining margin with a stable market share, or worse, a declining margin in conjunction with a declining market share, is a very significant early warning factor.

FINANCIAL MEASURES

The Z-score described earlier is not a bad aggregate indicator of financial health, particularly for a public company. It is not quite as appropriate for subsidiaries of quoted companies or for private companies because it includes a term which reflects the market value of the equity. However, the other terms in the Z-score calculation are still worth monitoring as a permanent test of company viability.

More conventionally cash flow is a key item to monitor, particularly cash flow measured against expected cash requirements, and cash flow measured against liabilities. As a component of this, the unvarnished profitability figures are very important. (By unvarnished I mean without any of the creative accounting fictions that are so easy to find in modern businesses.) The profitability numbers should be looked at in a context of items such as interest cover and of course its own volatility. In looking at both profitability and cash flow, it is worth considering what sort of risk exposure exists. This can include conventional risk exposure such as commodity positions that can be hedged, but also the operating risk of the company, measured by the ratio of its aggregate margin to breakeven level.

All these measures are taken as internal analysis, either because they require information available only to company management or alternatively because they involve a very high level of study and understanding of the industry, which is likely to be carried out only by the managers of the company, and not by observers of it. Accordingly, these measures are not as tested as some of the external financial measures, and of course they apply to very different time scales (the strategic measures look a long way into the future whilst the financial measures deal with the coming year or two). Nevertheless, exercised with proper judgement they can be very informative warning signals of problems to come.

CHAPTER 3

Feasibility analysis

■

Once it is clear that a company is at risk of financial collapse the key question is whether or not it can be rescued. Whether or not a decision can be made with any confidence depends entirely upon the information available to the decision maker. However, irrespective of the confidence level a decision *must* be made. If a company fits the screening mechanisms discussed so far, then inactivity will simply be fatal. The business trends and patterns of behaviour that are bleeding away the cash will continue, the liquidation value of the company will drop towards or below zero, and interests of the lenders, the investors, the employees, the suppliers and the customers will all be severely damaged. Bankruptcy is never pleasant.

Strategic audit

The amount of information available about a problem company is critical to making a valid decision. If a company is a subsidiary, then vast quantities of data are likely to be available. Management accounts, technical reports, personnel records, even (or perhaps especially) sales representatives' call reports can and should be raided. At this stage information is required firstly about the company itself and secondly about the company's environment – its competitors and its markets. For the company the following sources of data are likely to prove rewarding.

ACCOUNTING DATA

At the very least there should be a profit and loss account, a balance sheet and a cash flow statement, possibly with a capital expenditure and commitments statement. If a company is a subsidiary, or if perhaps it is up for sale, management accounts, budgets and plans may be available.

Since failure of control is one of the principal causes of corporate collapse, unaudited accounts should be treated with some circumspection; nevertheless something can be gleaned from them.

The issues to assess from the accounts are trends and/or sudden changes in sales volume, gross and net margins, cost by as many categories as possible and, of course, prices. Competent ratio analyses (see Fig. 3.1 and Fig. 3.2) and intelligent use of comparative analyses with previous years can be very informative (see Table 3.1). Given the raw data, ratio analysis over a sufficient period is a very good method of analysing problems back to their root cause. Similarly, a fund's flow statement would be extraordinarily valuable. Most particularly at this point we want to know what the cash has been used for and whether there has been a positive operating cash flow, which has been dissipated, or perhaps a worsening negative cash flow.

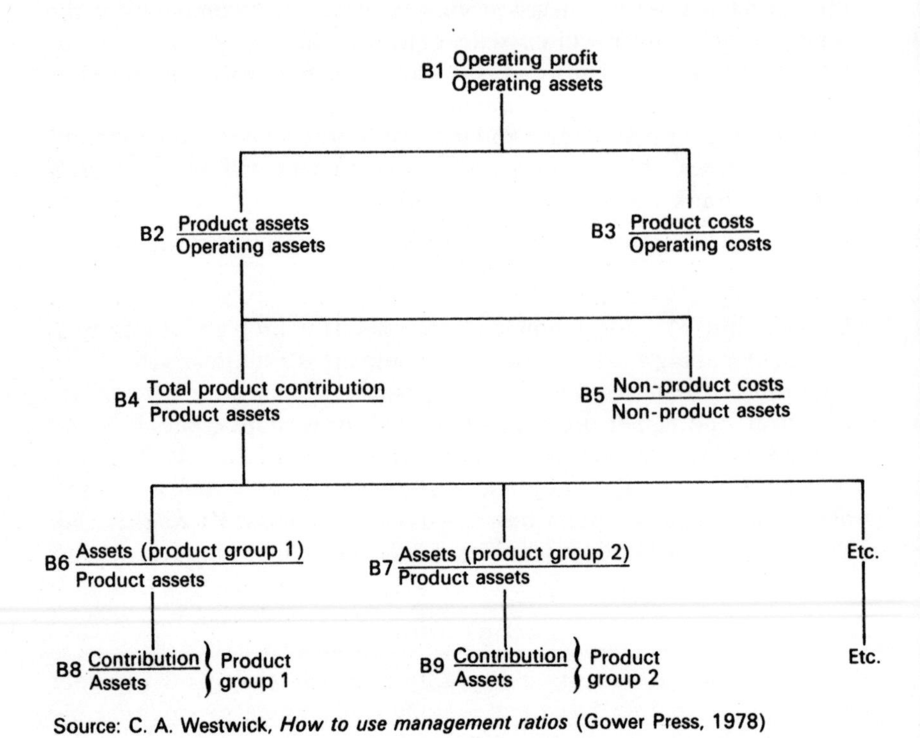

Source: C. A. Westwick, *How to use management ratios* (Gower Press, 1978)

Fig. 3.1. Product profitability analysis by ratio.

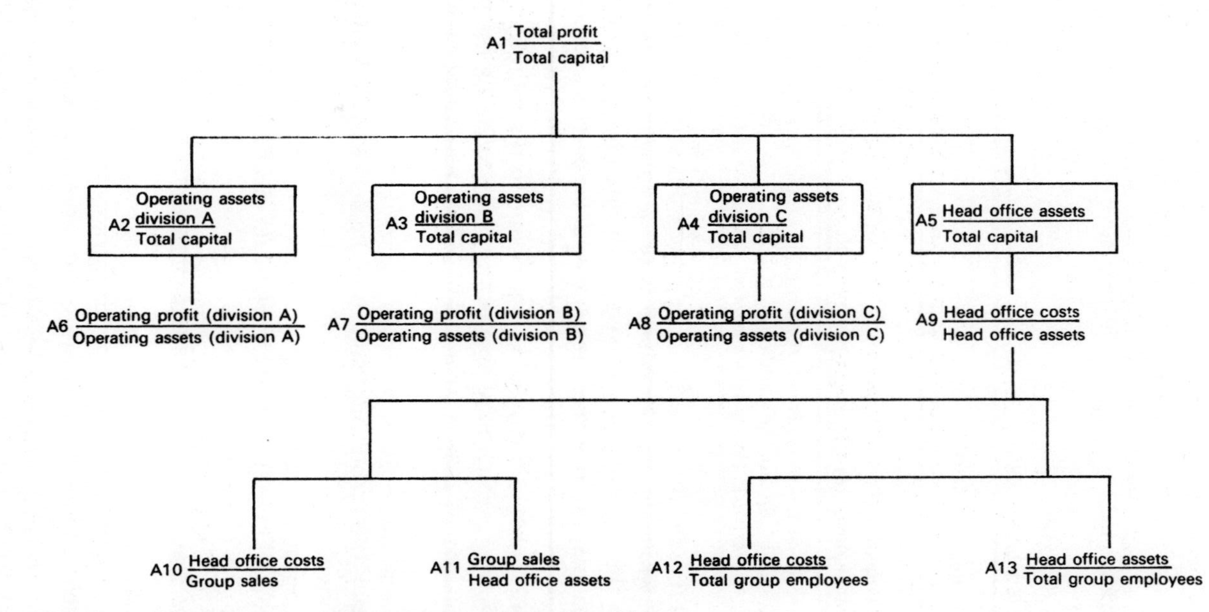

Source: C. A. Westwick, *How to use management ratios* (Gower Press, 1978)

Fig. 3.2. Divisionalised company: performance analysis by ratio.

Table 3.1. Simple ratios for preliminary analysis

Ratio	Year −5	−4	−3	−2	−1	Now
Profits as % of capital employed						
Profits as % of sales						
Sales as a multiple of capital employed						
Sales as a multiple of fixed assets						
Sales as a multiple of stocks						
Sales per employee (£)						
Profits per employee (£)						

Note: These simple ratios are actually those used by Arnold Weinstock in the days when he was bringing GEC up into the world class.
Source: C. A. Westwick, *How to use management ratios* (Gower Press, 1978).

In all these matters the three key questions should always be asked: 'where, when and why?' 'Where' may identify one or more key black spots in the organisation. Disposal or closure of such black spots, grim though it may be, may save the more valuable parts of a company. At the very least identifying these enables us to identify the healthy 'core' business. 'When did it start' is a guideline to three things. It helps us answer 'why', which may give us the route to curing the problem. It may also help us answer 'who did it', which will lead us to identify our weaker management. It also tells us how long things have been going wrong, and therefore how badly run down the organisation is.

All told, the accounting data should give us two insights. Firstly, it should give us our best clue as to how much time we have to effect the rescue. Secondly, it will give us a series of clues as to the causes of the problem, although this case can be by no means conclusive.

BANKERS AND LENDERS

Unless we have enormous resources and are willing to bring them to bear in support of this company, the people who have loaned money to our problem company will feature very large in our calculations. At this point the critical issue is to understand their attitudes and expectations. Are they concerned about the state of the company and the safety of their loan to it? Are they happy to wait for the outcome of the rescue attempt? Are they willing to lend more money to preserve what they have? Are they getting nervous and ready to cut and run? These issues will feature large when we come to consider the viability of the operation.

CUSTOMERS

These are perhaps the best source of insight into the reasons for a company's poor fortune. Their experience and beliefs (whether or not they are true) will dictate how much a company can sell in the market and at what price. If the product is important to the customers, then likely their purchasing managers and technical managers will be acutely conscious of the virtues and the drawbacks of the company's products, its sales force, its technical support, and indeed most aspects of its commercial policy. They will also measure these things against the only criterion that matters, namely how well the company meets the customers' requirements by comparison with the competition.

The only drawback with questioning customers is that to openly go out and talk about the company in such terms may put the problem company in further jeopardy. It is of course always possible to use consultants to carry out the survey and to render the questions anonymous. If the company makes consumer products it is often quite informative to look at reports from the consumer associations. These are generally quite influential and virtually always honest and well researched. If the product is too small to be of importance to the end customer, then one must talk to the merchant or retailer who handles the product in higher volume.

OTHER QUANTITATIVE DATA

Other quantitative data fall into two categories. If we have an insider's perspective, likely a large quantity of information abounds, although it may well be poorly presented, or even not seen at all. With companies in decline information systems from their better days often continue to operate, but nobody uses them. Sales data and technical data frequently exist buried within the organisation. Other sources of quantitative data are trade associations and occasionally sponsoring government departments (see Tables 3.2 and 3.3). These will frequently give market size and market share information.

Table 3.2. Trade associations and economic development councils in the UK that organise exchanges of information

(The following organisations carry out comparative surveys and/or exchanges of information in their industries or trades. The list is arranged in alphabetical order of industry.)

Institute of Practitioners in ADVERTISING
Scottish AGRICULTURAL Colleges
Ministry of AGRICULTURE, Fisheries and Food
Ministry of AGRICULTURE for Northern Ireland
British BRUSH Manufacturers' Research Association
National Federation of BUILDERS' and Plumbers Merchants
Institute of BUILDING
British CAST Iron Research Association
CHEMICAL Industries Association
COAL Tar Research Association
British CONSTRUCTIONAL Steelwork Association
National Association of DROP Forgers and Stampers
DYERS and Cleaners Research Organisation
Institute of FOOD Distribution
FURNITURE Development Council/Furniture Industry Research Association
British GLASS Industry Research Association
GLASS Manufacturers' Federation
Scottish GROCERS' Federation
HEATING and Ventilating Contractors' Association
National HOSIERY Manufacturers' Federation
HOT Dip Galvanisers Association
Institute of IRON and Steel Wire Manufacturers
National Federation of IRONMONGERS
Association of JUTE Spinners and Manufacturers
LEAD Development Association
LINEN Industry Research Association
MACHINE Tool Trades Association
MILK Marketing Board
MOTOR Agents Association
NEWSPAPER Society
PIRA: Research Association for the PAPER Board, Printing and Packaging Industries
PIG Industry Development Authority
National PORTS Council
British Federation of Master PRINTERS
Society of Master PRINTERS OF Scotland
Scottish RETAIL Drapers' Association
National Association of RETAIL Furnishers
RUBBER and Plastics Research Association of Great Britain
SCIENTIFIC Instrument Manufacturers' Association of Great Britain
SIRA (British SCIENTIFIC Instrument Research Association)
British SHIP Research Association
SHOE and Allied Trades Research Association
British SPINNERS' and DOUBLERS' Association

Table 3.2. (continued)

British STATIONERY and Office Equipment Association
TEXTILE Council Productivity Centre
TIMBER Trade Federation of the United Kingdom
Scottish TOURIST Industry Consultancy Service
Institute of Road TRANSPORT Engineers
British VALVE Manufacturers' Association

Source: C. A. Westwick, *How to use management ratios* (Gower Press, 1978).

Table 3.3. List of industries, trades, services and professions in which the Centre for Interfirm Comparison has conducted studies

Abattoirs
Academic libraries
Adoption services
Aluminium anodisers
Aluminium home improvement systems
Automatic vending
Bedding manufacture
Biscuit manufacture
Blanket manufacture
Book publishing
Book publishers' distribution
Breweries: managed houses
: tenanted houses' rents
Builders' merchants
Building and civil engineering
Bulk liquid haulage contractors
Carpet manufacture (a) woven
(b) tufted
Charities
Chemical manufacture*
Clothing manufacture
Cold rolled sections manufacture
Colour makers
Comparison of firms' performance in different geographical areas
Computing bureaux
Computing costs of large organisations
Corn and agricultural merchants
Cotton spinning
Crane manufacture
Credit card finance
Decorators' merchants
Distribution of food and consumer goods*
Domestic central heating equipment manufacture
Drop forgers
Electrical contractors
Electrical/electronic product manufacturers
Electrical engineering
Engineers' tool manufacture
English woollen and worsted industry
Express carriers
Finance houses
Flexible package manufacture
Food distribution
Forgemasters
Fork lift truck manufacture
Gauge and tool manufacture
Glass container manufacture
Hand tool manufacture
Hotels
Housing associations
Industry in new towns
Invoicing and credit control
Iron foundries
Joinery manufacture
Leather dressing
Local authority services
Machine tool importers
Machine tool manufacture
Mains cable manufacture
Maintenance costs in manufacturing industry*
Marketing research
Mechanical engineering*

Table 3.3. (continued)

Narrow fabric manufacture
Non-ferrous foundries
Nylon hose dyeing
Painting and decorating contractors
Paintmakers
Paper manufacture
Paper sack manufacture
Passenger transport systems
Periodical publishers
Pharmaceutical manufacture
Pipework contractors
Plastics moulding
Public libraries
Pump manufacture
Radio and electronic component manufacture
Raw materials' costs
Rayon weaving
Residential homes for the elderly
Resin manufacture
Road haulage*
Rubber manufacture*
Scientific instrument manufacture
Scottish woollen industry
Secondary aluminium ingots
Shirt manufacture
Soft drinks manufacture
Solicitors, in conjunction with The Law Society
Steel stockholders
Stockbrokers
Structural steelwork
Tank and industrial plant manufacture
Throwsters
Tie manufacture
Timber importers
Timber merchants
Valve manufacture (mechanical)
Veterinary practices
Vehicle recovery operators
Wallcovering manufacture
Warp knitting
Water authorities

* Covering various types and size groups
Source: The Centre for Interfirm Comparison (August 1987).

PRESS – TRADE AND GENERAL

The trade press in most industries carries a phenomenal amount of useful qualitative information, often in the 'who's doing what to whom' category. Contracts won and lost, new people taking over jobs, old people losing jobs, all feature large. Again, the trade press informs on what the competition is doing and what is happening to the market in general. The press in general is quite a good source in this respect, and of course with more and more being accessible via electronic databases, the process of searching for qualitative information is becoming a practical and indeed an economical proposition.

This first stage of attacking a problem company is all about gleaning clues from incomplete, partial, and occasionally partisan data. It is a task that is actually becoming easier over time, as information technology improves in all its data-handling aspects. Almost by the day databases become more competent and more comprehensive. The spreadsheet software enables detailed modelling of the internal mechanics of companies in a way simply not possible ten years ago. Today the would-be company rescuer ignores such technology at his peril.

Outline plan

To assess whether to undertake a company rescue, one must make judgements on what is achievable. The best way to do this is to determine broadly what is necessary to render the company viable and draw up an outline plan to that end. However, for any plan to work, it is essential to have the following:

1. A viable base business.
2. Adequate resources.
3. Highly competent new management or leadership.
4. Proper authority in the hands of the new management.
5. Investor commitment.

Each of these areas is treated in some detail in the sections that follow.

THE VIABILITY OF THE BASE BUSINESS

The company needs to have two quite independent sorts of viability in order to be a good rescue prospect. It is rather like a medical patient who has a sickness that is terminal without treatment. The two conditions for his survival are that the condition is treatable and that he is strong enough to survive the treatment or operation required. Similarly, a company has to be capable of being a successful competitor in its market place in the long term, but it also has to be able to survive long enough to become successful once again.

Short-term survival

Short-term viability is virtually entirely a matter of assets, liabilities and cash flow. Comerford, looking at the US experience, found he could predict those companies that would survive two years after going into their old Chapter Eleven bankruptcy proceedings.[13] Comerford's analysis like Altman's looked at characteristics such as net income over assets, total debt over total assets, quick assets to total assets, current assets to current liabilities, quick assets to current liabilities, and net income to shareholders' equity. This is the old story of measuring the resources of the company against the rate at which those resources drain away; the logic explicitly assessed by Jarrod Wilcox's gamblers' ruin model. If the company failed Comerford's screen, then it had an 80% chance of not surviving two years. If it passed his screen, it had a nearly 90% chance of surviving that period.

The first point of analysis, therefore, is the balance sheet. Using

Wilcox's rule of three-quarters of current assets and half of fixed assets book values, but measuring debt and creditors at full value, how much liquidity do we have left? At the current rate of loss of liquidity, in terms of negative cash flow and in terms of working capital needs, how much time do we have left before the business is valueless? Once this analysis has been done, we can address ways of stretching this time span. This step is to identify areas where the rate of haemorrhage can be reduced. These might be as follows:

1. If parts of the business are losing large quantities of money, they can be sold off or closed down. The trade-off then is between costs of closure versus costs of on-going operation.
2. If parts of the business are using large quantities of money (for a capital expenditure programme, for example), or using very large quantities of working capital as a proportion of sales and in relation to profits, identify where the capital programme can be stopped, the use of working capital made more efficient, or the sales expansion stopped.
3. Look at the asset base of parts of the business in relation to the returns made on those parts. The critical measurement here is the return on capital employed, where capital employed is the working capital at full value, and fixed assets at disposal value rather than book value. It is surprising how often a moribund, undercapitalised and obsolete factory is sitting on a location worth many times its book value. This is quite often the case with older factories situated near major city centres.

It may be that such actions would actually create stability in the company, although by themselves they are unlikely to constitute a complete turnaround in the company's fortune. What they will do is give the company time; and on a rough basis we will be able to calculate how much time they allow for the rescue proper to take effect.

The next judgement to make is whether this time is sufficient. As a rule anything closer than two years of the company failing to zero value is too little and too late unless we are willing to inject capital of our own. Some actions have a more rapid impact than others, however. Cost reductions, rationalisations, and asset realisations are relatively fast to implement, unless a large proportion of the savings involves labour cost reduction.

It is always important to look closely at the negotiating structures and at the character of the unions involved. Where a long history of unionisation exists, particularly in low-growth, highly capital intensive, high market share businesses – and therefore very strong negotiators and trade unions that are used to getting their own way – these strategies may take rather longer. Nevertheless, they are still feasible,as British Steel and Jaguar demonstrate (albeit with the initial advantage of the infinite banking capacity of the British government).

On the sales front, it may be possible to implement a quick price increase, particularly to products that are infrequently purchased, low as a proportion of buyers' total expenditures, highly differentiated or already have a very high margin. Such products are least likely to be price sensitive and most likely to maintain volume.

These are the quick-return actions. It takes somewhat longer to get significant productivity improvements (except in cases of extreme slackness), and much longer for quality improvements, service improvements, product improvements and design innovations. Accordingly, plans that need these component actions are feasible only for companies with enough resources to last a few years.

Given this brief analysis it should become clear whether a business has time available to it to take the actions necessary for long-term survival. Armed with this knowledge, and indeed some notion of how that time will be used, we must talk to the lenders and creditors of the business. If, as is probable, they have been unnerved by the behaviour of the business to date, they will welcome such an approach. If they do, and they seem willing to give the company sufficient time to recover, then we have the beginnings of viability.

Warm words are not enough, however. Other firmer agreements must be made before undertaking the exercise; and indeed it may be possible, if room for manoeuvre is extremely tight, to negotiate interest holidays, write-offs or repayment deferrals, all of which will give the company that much more chance of survival. It is essential to have a financial plan to support the business action plan.

Long-term viability of the business

Many company rescuers manage to stave off the evil day. It is not uncommon, however, for such short-term actions to leave the company either foundering in profitability that is too low to regenerate its capital or indeed to repay its investors. Given the effort, the stress and the risk inherent in a rescue attempt, this sort of turnaround may not be worth what one puts into it. Inadequate outcomes can be caused by poor recovery strategy, by poor implementation or by the company being incapable of maintaining viability because of its history, its location and the business it is in. It is important, therefore, to make at least some assessment of this last factor, the long-term viability of the business, before undertaking the effort of the rescue.

Three elements determine the long-term viability of a business:

1. The industrial structure.
2. The market environment.
3. The operating effectiveness of the company.

Each of these issues is addressed in the sections that follow.

Industrial structure

The last ten years has witnessed enormous strides in the understanding of what makes an industry profitable or unprofitable. A great deal of empirical evidence has been gathered by the Strategic Planning Institute in the Profit Impact of Market Strategy (PIMS) database.[14] In addition, a very high level of analytical insight has been cast on the whole issue by the guru of the field, Michael Porter.[15] The essence of Porter's argument is that the profitability within an industry is determined by five factors, namely:

1. The bargaining power of the buyers.
2. The bargaining power of suppliers.
3. The threat of substitute products or services.
4. The threat of new entrants to the industry.
5. The rivalry amongst existing firms.

In Porter's words:

> The collective strength of these five competitive forces determines the ability of firms in industry to earn, on average, rates of return on investment in excess of the costs of capital. The strength of the five forces varies from industry to industry, and can change as an industry evolves. The result is that all industries are not alike from the standpoint of inherent profitability. In industries where the five forces are favourable, such as pharmaceuticals, soft drinks, and database publishing, many competitors earn attractive returns. But in industries where pressure from one or more of the forces is intense, as in rubber, steel, and video games, few firms command attractive returns, despite the best efforts of management. Industry profitability is not a function of what a product looks like, or whether it embodies high or low technology, but of industry structure. Some very mundane industries such as postage meters and grain trading are extremely profitable, whilst the more glamorous high technology industries such as personal computers and cable television are not profitable for many participants.[16]

This model, and the factors that determine the level of competition created by the various negotiating relationships outlined by Porter, are summarised in Fig. 3.3.

Unlike many of the themes that sweep through management from time to time, this framework has a great deal of empirical evidence to support it, both of the anecdotal case study form, and also in the enormously detailed statistical analysis to be found in the PIMS database. The three issues that have to be addressed by the would-be company rescuer are as follows:

1. Is the industry currently profitable? This involves a reasonably detailed analysis of the industry structure.
2. Has there been a change in the industry structure that reduces the inherent profitability of the industry? Most particularly, is the cause of the rescue target's decline a major structural change? (e.g. are there any new entrants such as new Korean competitors; any new substitutes in the form of products created by new technologies; any increase in rivalry amongst competitors caused by new ownership in one of the major ones; any increase in bargaining leverage as a result of a trend towards merger on the part of buying firms, as happened in British retailing; any increases in supplier bargaining power such as happened initially with the cartelisation of oil supplies by OPEC.) If such a change is the cause of the target company's decline, then this probably represents the most difficult sort of rescue, since it involves either changing the structure of the industry (which is normally impossible) or more likely finding a whole new niche for the company to prosper in. This latter action is one of the most difficult tasks the management can undertake, most of all in an industry new to it.
3. On the basis of the proceeding analysis, what part of the industry offers the best scope for a highly profitable operation?

Market environment

The wider compass in which the competitive analysis is drawn is the environment. Key issues are the overall performance of the economy, both in terms of growth and inflation, and its implication for the markets the target company works in. The behaviour of those markets, whether they are on a downturn of a normally volatile behaviour, or whether they are on a downward secular trend is of course critical.

Donald Bibeault in his book on corporate turnarounds lists one in six turnarounds as so-called 'economic turnarounds'.[17] These recoveries barely qualify as company rescues, but they do indicate how important

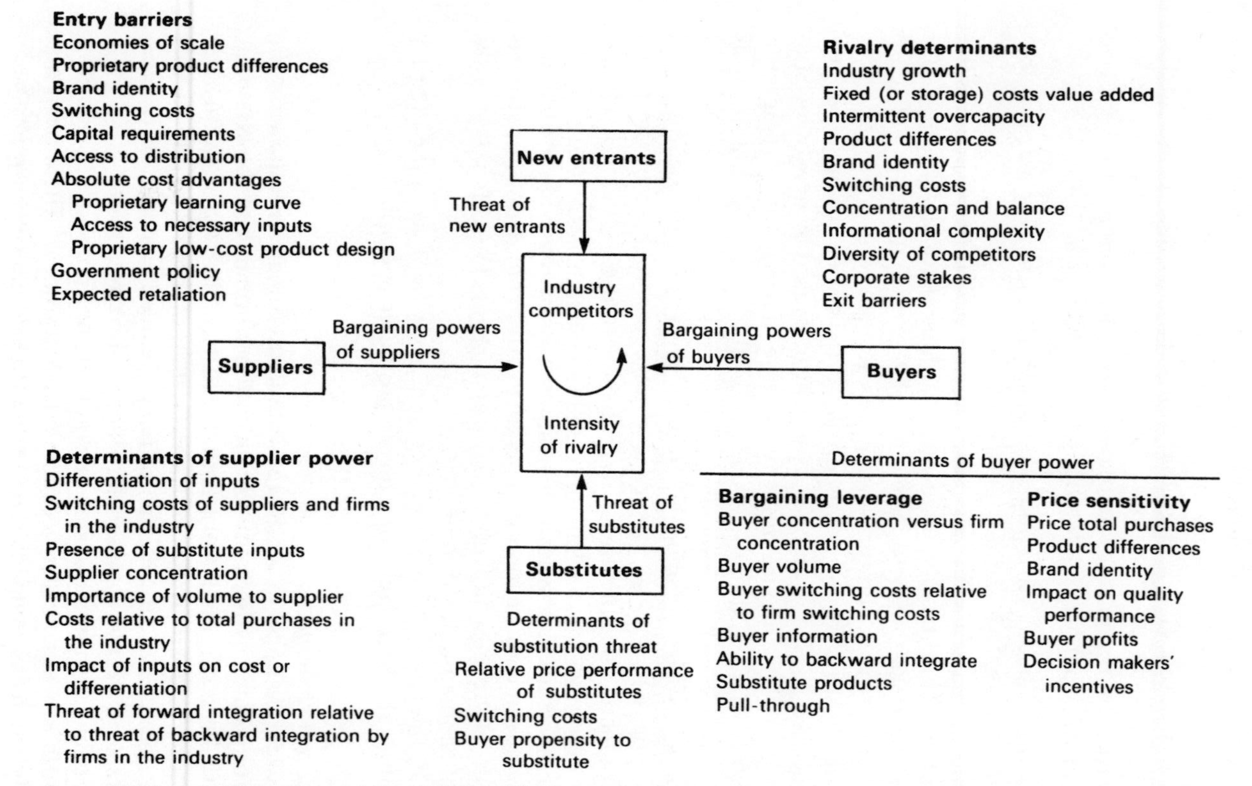

Fig. 3.3. Elements of industry structure.

the outside environment can be. There is no doubt that it is considerably easier to rescue a company in improving conditions than in other circumstances. Clearly an important part of the timing of many management buy-outs is that they are aimed to capitalise on an upturn in their own market.

Analysis of company operating effectiveness

At this point in the analysis whether the problem is principally an internal or external one should be clear. In particular it should be possible to identify whether the problem is one of cost runaway, volume loss, pricing and/or margin decline, or one of the many other external categories touched upon in Chapter 1.

Although they may not be known for certain, the original causes of the problem will become clear. Perhaps the previously successful company has not reacted quickly enough to a change in environment, and its old successful rules of thumb have now become a liability. It may be that the company has strayed into areas where it has weak skills; or it may have let its own basic skills decline under lax management over a long period. A correction of these original problems each carries its own class of difficulty. Long-term problems tend to imply poor management; as a corollary the more rapid and shorter term problems tend to mean that there is good management in place, albeit management that has to learn new rules. Each cause carries its own cure, which while not constituting a complete rescue will necessarily form part of the final strategy.

Ideally, one would like to be able to assess the strategic shape of the company at the end of the rescue period to determine what options are available. It would be best to be able to assess whether the company will aim to be a cost leader, a product-differentiated supplier, or a focused supplier. The reality is that at this stage that would be little more than a loose judgement. The best that can be hoped for is an assessment of the types of strategy that might be appropriate for the industry and whether the capability for such strategies exists within the target company. The real question now is to determine what strategic options are available for the immediate aftermath of purchase and in the first stages of the rescue attempt. Those strategic options are enumerated as follows:

1. *Financial restructuring.* The assessment of how much time is needed to rebuild the company, and how much time is available in the light of its balance sheet and cash flow forecasts, will lead to a judgement as to whether financial restructuring is necessary. This may involve

conversion of debt to equity, deferred repayment schedules, interest holidays, or even acceptance of write-offs by investors, lenders and creditors. Whether such matters are possible should be assessable from the interviews with each of these groups of people before undertaking the rescue attempt. In fact the most wise approach might well be to get these contractually agreed before any rescue attempt is started. Of course part of the rescue might involve the injection of a large proportion of new equity by the rescuing company itself.

2. *Realisation of underperforming saleable assets.* This is an area where they may be a great deal of information, particularly if the assets involve real estate. Estimation of proceeds from this should be straightforward. Much more difficult is a calculation of what might be realised from selling parts of the organisation as going concerns, to competitors or to other people than can add value. Nevertheless, one should be able to make a rough-and-ready assessment.
3. *Scope for immediate rationalisation.* Closure of badly haemorrhaging parts of the business is the most brutal approach, but it is also the fastest, the most predictable, and often the most effective way of protecting the core of the business.
4. *Scope for rapid cost reduction.* The issues with this short-term strategy are those of size and timing. Wage reductions can of course be achieved by redundancies, wage cuts, or wage freezes. Negotiating timetables on such things are notoriously difficult to predict, but in the circumstances of a failing company they can sometimes be extremely rapid, and remarkably large in magnitude. Again, this is a harsh solution, but often an effective one. Similar negotiations can be addressed to suppliers, particularly those that depend on the target company for a major part of their business. Faced with the prospect of losing a large proportion of their sales, they may well be forthcoming with significant improvements in cost.
5. *Scope for a radical increase in sales revenue.* This is almost always the slowest portion of the immediate recovery strategy. The easiest increase comes from putting up prices, but this of course may have severe side effects in the commercial area in terms of loss of volume and loss of market share. In assessing this strategy it is worth looking at the extent to which the company's product is differentiated, the switching costs of the customer, how significant the item is to the customer in terms of the proportion of its total cost, and indeed the margin that already exists on the product (high-margin products are often easier to increase in price than are low-margin products).

Increases in volumes are generally achievable by improvements in products, improvements in sales force effectiveness, and improvements in the general marketing mix. However, product improvements are invariably slow. Even the most effective of them – improvements in quality – take at least a year to have an impact. Improvements in sales forces, like any reorganisations, are invariably slow starters, and changes in advertising and distribution channels are unreliable and hazardous.

Also not to be forgotten is that unlike all the other areas, changes in approaches to marketing frequently precipitate a competitor response that may be very dangerous indeed. It is useful to know whether the competition has enough spare capacity to take away a significant proportion of our market share.

ADEQUATE RESOURCES

At this stage, assessing what resources are needed to bring about this rescue and whether the rescuing concern has them is most important. The would-be rescuer must determine the financial requirements as well as the personnel requirements.

Finance

The easiest area to assess is finance, although the classical mistake is to underestimate quite how expensive and how long the recovery process could be. Unusually in business this is one area where capital rationing really does apply, so it is critical to get this calculation right.

Personnel

The most difficult judgement of all is in selecting personnel. Successful rescues almost invariably require highly competent new leadership in the form of a new chief executive. They frequently need partial replacement of the second tier and sometimes, albeit quite infrequently, they need complete replacement of the second tier. This latter circumstance is extremely risky indeed. The new chief executive will be critical to the operation of the company in a way that no other chief executive is. He will need to exercise hands-on management with absolute authority, and be capable of operating extremely tight controls. He will need to be a first-class negotiator. He will also need to be a first-class leader in the sense that he will need to motivate demoralised or apathetic, or even hostile, people to do a job they probably think is impossible. He will also need a broad base of business experience or a very broad base of training to give him the wide knowledge of business technicalities needed to bring the company around. Ideally he will also need to have experience in the industry concerned. Finally, in a perfect world he will need to come from within the organisation of the rescuing concern, since spotting such a paragon by the interview process is unlikely to be successful.

The second possible issue, the whole or partial replacement of the second tier, is a little less difficult. In any successful rescue it will be critically important to have three strong leaders beneath the chief executive, one in each of the financial, operational, and marketing functions. Since failure of financial control is a frequent cause of business collapse, a replacement of the finance director or financial vice-president is a very common and very necessary part of the rescue procedure. Nevertheless, it should not reduce the importance of the operational and marketing heads, particularly if the chief executive does not have specific industry skills, for it is these specific skills that are principally found in the operational and marketing departmental heads.

INVESTOR COMMITMENT

Rescues are invariably trying exercises, both from an emotional and a financial point of view. Along the way there are frequently setbacks and disappointments, and plenty of occasions for despair. It is not therefore an exercise to be undertaken under any misapprehensions or any false sense of pride.

Some are of the view that only one in four collapsing companies recovers. Nonetheless, there are good reasons to undertake rescues. Failing companies frequently come cheap but can, in a successful outcome, become very profitable. In addition, one should not forget that even the most successful companies have their bad years. This is true even of the sample of some 70 publicly quoted mid-size companies with phenomenally high growth rates on which Donald Clifford and Richard Cavanagh based their book *The winning performance*; indeed, in that sample of 70 companies, 28 showed a loss in at least 1 year in the last 20.[18] A company rescue is nevertheless a difficult process and should not be undertaken without significant determination and confidence in the final outcome.

A part of this commitment and confidence should be a willingness to put proper authority in the hands of the rescue specialist who becomes the chief executive of the target company. If the rescuing concern is not willing to do this, which in effect means handing over virtually absolute power, then it should not start the exercise. Nothing destroys rescues more effectively than an attempt to run them by committee through a board of directors worrying about every penny of its investment.

Is it worth it to us?

To the rescuing concern it should be clear whether the target company is capable of survival in the short term and strategically worthwhile in the long term. The next questions then are 'is our concern the best operation to undertake this rescue? Do we have the necessary technical skills? Do we have the necessary chief executive in-house? Do we have the necessary determination and financial resources to carry it through? Are there other companies that have a better portfolio of characteristics that fit this requirement?'

CONCLUSION

The options available are therefore as follows:

1. Close the company and liquidate its assets.
2. Sell the company as a going concern.
3. Undertake a rescue attempt.

If it is not a good survival candidate in the short term, or its long-term strategic viability looks doubtful, then the most sensible option is to close the company and liquidate its assets. Rarely is this true for every part of a company, and in the interests of preserving the jobs of the employees, and value for the investors, lenders and creditors, an attempt should be made to sell at least parts of it as going concerns. However, the option of selling should be looked at seriously with a company that is viable in the long term but either needs too much cash to help it survive the short term or has a viability that is dependent upon too many skills that are unavailable to our own concern. If all these hurdles have been passed, then it is with a reasonable degree of confidence that one may undertake the rescue of the target company.

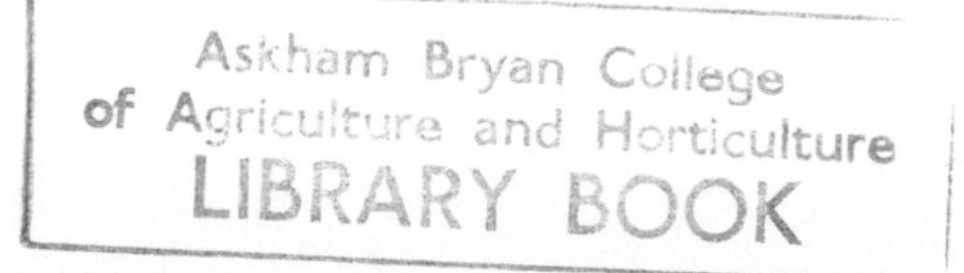

CHAPTER 4

The new chief executive

■

Selecting the chief executive to carry out the rescue of the target company is probably the most difficult decision to be taken in the whole process. Personnel selection of any sort is a most chancy business, with failure rates frequently in excess of 50%. In this particular case it is doubly hazardous, for two reasons. Firstly, the skills required are extremely rare; they are not prerequisites to the running of a steady-state business, and are sometimes even destructive in that context. Therefore they are hard to find, and worse, hard to measure. The only really good test of a turnaround manager is that he has carried out a successful rescue before – and by its nature that combination is rare. Secondly, there is probably only one opportunity to get the decision right. If the company needs a rescue attempt, then it is unlikely to survive long enough to be allowed the luxury of a second chief executive.

There are several critical characteristics to look for in selecting the new chief executive. The man or woman we seek has to be unusually confident in three roles. He or she has to be a perceptive strategist, a master tactician, and a first-class leader.

Strategist

The best business strategists operate by a mixture of recognition and reflex, intuition and analysis. To achieve this they ideally have to have wide technical competence, understanding the operations, marketing, finance and organisation all tolerably well, along with broad business experience. This experience should include decision-making line experience. It is the case in military strategy that the best generals are officers who have experienced the smoke of battle at first hand and understand the difficulties and complexities of implementing theoretical strategies. Similarly, in business the strategies succeed or fail, as the Americans put it, 'when the rubber meets the road'. Turnarounds in particular fail more often in implementation than strategy. The manager will uniquely have to both devise and implement his own strategy and will therefore need to have the skills of turning the paper plan into concrete achievement.[19]

Ideally, the new leader should have industry-specific skills. He will, in the first six months of his tenure, have to make rapid decisions about highly complex market, operational and financial matters. He will have to challenge decisions of people who have been in the industry for many years. He will have to assess data that are unreliable, or just plain biased. He will have to establish new rules of thumb for the operation, different to the ones that got the company into problems in the first place. He will have to assess complex competitive challenges, and he will have to perceive and judge risks that other people do not even see. In all these areas industry experience is invaluable. It is also probably the case that the majority of successful company rescuers have some experience in the industry itself or in an industry allied to the one in which their company operates. There are, however, two caveats to this rule. The first is that such managers may not be available, least of all with all the other characteristics demanded of a turnaround specialist. Secondly, there is always a risk that somebody already in the industry is likely to be hide-bound by the rules of thumb that already operate within that industry. This risk is particularly salient when the cause of the company failure is a new external competitive threat. Under these circumstances, at the very least, an outsider should be considered.

Commendation of such general-purpose paragons of virtue as the 'all-purpose generalist' are of little value in the real world, however, where real decisions have to be taken. It will undoubtedly be the case that the choices available will be more strong in some areas and less strong in others. The analysis so far will have shown weaknesses in the failing company in one or more of the areas of finance, operations and marketing. If the failure is in finance (in its broadest sense of including management accounting and control), then in addition to a new chief executive the company will probably need a new financial head. The new chief executive, therefore, does not need to be a financial specialist, although numeracy should be a mandatory requirement. If the weakness is in operations or marketing, however, it is worthwhile favouring candidates who have strengths in those areas (although not at the expense of having no knowledge in the other areas).

The new man must be intensely data orientated. Once he arrives in the failing company, he will find no shortage of opinions as to what caused the failure. Plenty of people will have axes to grind. Every department will think every other department is to blame. The problem facing the new chief executive is that in the midst of all this noise will be some nuggets of truth, and he will have to sift through all these confusing opinions to find the hard facts. Amidst these combinations of self-delusion and self-protective deception the new manager will have few reference points. The information systems will be poor, or if they are competent they are likely to be measuring the wrong things. Despite this the rescue specialist must be persistent in his pursuit of the facts. He will probably be installing new information systems within short order, but he will also be forever checking and corroborating what he has been told against whatever hard data he finds.

Few rescue specialists qualify as academic intellectuals, yet the rescue specialist must be analytical and innovative. Analytical in the sense that he will have to pin down the overall causes of the company's failure and decide on the strategies for the correction. Innovative in the sense that he will always be making changes in every area of the company's activity, for example, in new production methods, new supplier contracts, new incentives, new types of customer relationship, new levels of achievement. All these areas and many others need the peculiar blend of imagination and courage that goes into making a good innovator.

Professor John Kotter of the Harvard Business School undertook a long study of what made successful general managers different from unsuccessful ones, and he described it in a brilliantly successful book entitled *The General Manager*. One of the key points he identified was that successful general managers operated initially on very loose, ill-defined (and therefore error-tolerant) plans. In creating the plan, or agenda, they turned to an enormous number of different sources of information. Kotter contrasts this method with the conventional formal planning process as follows:

> First, the formal plans tend to be written mostly in terms of detailed financial numbers. General Managers' agendas tend to be less detailed in financial objectives and more detailed in strategies and plans for the business or the organisation.
>
> Second, formal plans usually focus entirely on the short and moderate run (3 months to 6 years), while General Managers' agendas tend to focus on a broader time frame, which includes the immediate future (1 to 30 days) and the longer run (5 to 20 years).
>
> Finally, the formal plans tend to be more explicit, rigorous, and logical,

especially regarding how various financial items fit together. General Managers' agendas often contain lists of goals or plans that are not as explicitly connected.

Executives begin the process of developing these agendas immediately after starting their jobs, if not before. They use their knowledge of the businesses and organisations involved along with new information received each day to quickly develop a rough agenda – typically this contains a very loosely connected and incomplete set of objectives, along with a few specific strategies and plans. Then over time, as more and more information is gathered, they incrementally (one step at a time) make the agendas more complete and more tightly connected.

In gathering information to set their agendas, effective General Managers rely more on discussions with others than on books, magazines, or reports. These people tend to be individuals with whom they have relationships, not necessarily people in the 'appropriate' job or function (e.g. such as a person in the planning function). In this way they obtain information continuously, day after day, not just at planning meetings. And they do so by using their current knowledge of the business and organisation and of management in general to help them direct their questioning, not by asking broad or general questions. In other words, they find ways within the flow of their workdays to ask a few critical questions and to receive in return some information that would be useful for agenda-setting purposes.

With this information, General Managers make agenda-setting decisions both consciously (or analytically) and unconsciously (or intuitively) in a process that is largely internal to their minds. Indeed, important agenda-setting decisions are often not observable. In selecting specific activities to include in their agendas, General Managers look for those that accomplish multiple goals, that are consistent with all other goals and plans, and that are within their power to implement. Projects and programs that seem important and logical but do not meet these criteria tend to be discarded or are at least resisted.

Almost all effective General Managers seem to use this type of agenda-setting process, but the best performers do so to a greater degree and with more skill. For example, the 'excellent' performers I have studied develop agendas based on more explicit business strategies that address longer time frames and that include a wider range of business issues. They do so by more aggressively seeking information from others (including 'bad news'), by more skillfully asking questions, and by more successfully seeking out programs and projects that can help accomplish multiple objectives at once.[20]

Accurate identification of this style of behaviour, and selection on this basis, is difficult indeed. Yet it is even more crucial to a rescue specialist than to a conventional general manager, for it forms part of his information gathering, strategy formulation, control, and personnel-testing process.

Tactician

Primarily, the rescue expert must have the entrepreneurial instinct and skills to use opportunities that situations deliver to him, and also to create the situations that deliver those opportunities. Further, he must have expert negotiating skills. Indeed, these two skills together have strategic as well as tactical importance. The rescue specialist will have many 'tactical' negotiations to make, starting with a negotiation that is necessary to establish the financial resources of the company to carrying through negotiations with suppliers, workforce and customers. A great deal of modern business strategy also involves positioning companies in such a way as to optimise their negotiating leverage. An ability to drive a hard bargain, and an ability to understand how negotiations work and how to set them up, is critical to the new chief executive.

Decisiveness is self-evidently a necessary characteristic also, but the new man must be capable of *bold* decision, not just decisiveness. When he comes into the organisation, the new chief executive will need to do things that will allow him to seize the initiative in running the company. His actions will be visible, salient, and often against the conventional wisdom of everybody else around him. If he makes the wrong decisions, if he fails, everyone will say 'I told you so'. For this reason he will also have to be right.

He will need to be able to concentrate on clear targets and keep those targets in view no matter what the distractions and noise. And when those targets are broken down into subordinate objectives for his personnel, he will need to understand clearly the implications of failure to achieve any of those objectives for his strategic targets. His commitment to action and results will border on the fanatical. Accordingly, he will be a 'hands-on' manager, or at least capable of being so. He will put a great deal of emphasis on tight controls and be comfortable with their operation. This means inevitably a forceful character, since rigorous control systems suffer their own sort of entropy: they become flaccid and collapse as soon as the chief executive allows them to do so.

Thus, the manager will have certain characteristics not within today's conventional wisdom. He will have or develop a network of hundreds, maybe thousands, of people to call upon at regular intervals for assistance, support, advice and information. Kotter[21] describes such network building in some detail, as follows:

In addition to setting agendas, effective General Managers allocate significant time and effort when they first take their jobs to developing a network of cooperative relationships among those people they feel are needed to satisfy their emerging agendas.

Generally it is most intense during the first months in a job.

This network-building activity is aimed at much more than just direct subordinates. General Managers develop cooperative relationships with and among peers, outsiders, their bosses' boss, and their subordinates' subordinates, with any and all of the hundreds or even thousands of people on whom they feel dependent because of their jobs.

Furthermore, they also sometimes shape their networks by trying to create certain types of relationships *among* the people in various parts of the network. That is, they try to create the appropriate 'environment' (norms and values) they feel is necessary to implement their agendas. Typically this is an environment in which people are willing to work hard on the GM's agenda and cooperate for the greater good. Although executives sometimes try to create such an environment among peers, bosses, or outsiders, they do so most often among their subordinates.

He will also demonstrate another characteristic that is perhaps even more surprising: he will be inconsistent. When managers of very high accomplishment are compared with managers of low accomplishment one of the key characteristics of the accomplishing managers is that they change their behaviour to that which is appropriate. Work carried out by Wickham Skinner and Earl Sasser at Harvard shows that in management the really high accomplishers try to make their behaviour appropriate to the task and situation, rather than consistent, and in so doing they vary the attributes shown in Table 4.1.

Skinner and Sasser describe executive style thus:

This is a big order. It says, 'Be different. Don't always manage the same way.' Yet only a few managers studied were able to accomplish this kind of self-control and discipline. Those who did acted intuitively for the most part and often prior experience influenced them to realise that different behaviour was called for in a particular new situation: 'I've got to be tougher, more decisive, faster paced, delegate more than usual.' Successful retooling and refocus of executive style appeared to be the most important change that might have turned failures to successes in the situations we studied.

Why this step is seldom carried out is due perhaps in part to these prevailing attitudes: 'You must be natural and do your thing in your own natural way.' 'A successful manager would be foolish to tinker with his or her style.' 'A good manager can manage anything and any situation.' Our analysis suggests that these notions are largely myths and that careful, honest experimentation with executive style is a tool of vast potential, seldom used.[22]

The only way to test for this characteristic reliably is to look at the

Table 4.1. Some attributes of an executive style

Attributes	Range/Continuum	
Analytical patterns	Intuitive	Analytical
Cognitive style	Inductive	Deductive, use of generalisations
Decision making	Authoritative	Consultative
Decision-making speed	Fast, quick	Studied, worried
Delegation	Little	Much
Explicit 'rules of thumb'	Few	Many
Type of follow-up	Loose, little	Much, rigorous
Communication	Informal, verbal	Formal, written
Personal relationships	Supportive	Demanding, challenging
Pressure, pace	Relaxed	Rigorous, energetic
Availability	Easily available	Remote
Boldness, audacity	Bold, risk taker	Cautious, risk aversive
Focus on time dimension	Seldom	Continuous
Openness to persuasion	Flexible	Dogged, persistent, single-minded
Work with subordinates	One on one	In a group
Work with superior	Wants support	Works alone

Source: Wickham Skinner, *Manufacturing: the formidable competitive weapon* (John Wiley, 1985).

would-be chief executive's previous activities and track record. If he has the required breadth of experience, he will have had to have used different styles of behaviour at different times. If evidence of the ability to make an appropriate and flexible response is lacking, then the candidate may be appropriate for one stage of the rescue (e.g. the first or crisis stage), but he will not be able to manage the transition to normal performance.

Leader

If the rescue attempt is properly organised, the new chief executive will in effect have absolute authority. And he must be capable of exercising that authority to the full effect, for even the most brilliant turnaround specialist will not be able to achieve his intended aim by himself. He will need to motivate the people within the organisation to deliver performance for him. He will need to be able to mobilise their emotional and intellectual capacities over the whole organisation and stimulate them into a burst of creative energy they have rarely if ever experienced before. To achieve this will almost certainly involve a visible style of leadership (a more detailed review of leadership requirements and techniques is covered in Chapter 5). The leader will need charisma: his personality, his power and his strength will need to be such that they attract loyalty and inspire achievement – and this will involve a deal of audacity, conviction, and aplomb. In addition, the leader must be able to demand high standards of performance. Many who have not lived through a rescue might expect the failing organisation to resent this demand. Yet if anything, the reverse is true. There is of course a winnowing out of those who cannot keep pace, but those remaining get great satisfaction in their new-found success. With frequent fulfilment they acquire an appetite for more success. Again, this is a characteristic most easily tested in performance. If a leader has working for him many people who seem to thrive on the success, and enjoy the pressure and demands he puts upon them, then he has what it takes to effect the rescue.

The corollary of demanding high standards of performance is that the turnaround specialist must discriminate enormously among his employees. This discrimination is based solely upon how much an employee can help the task in hand. Inevitably, the leader must favour those who promise what he needs, and deliver on their promises. A willingness to support competent subordinates but not tolerate incompetent or lazy ones is an important part of fulfilling the rescue mission. Thus the ideal candidate will typically have a history that shows a sharp increase in subordinate turnover at the beginning of a task as he winnows out the non-performers, followed by a period of greater than normal stability because of the loyalty of the high performers. This is difficult to detect after the event, but one marker is a high proportion of subordinates who started employment with the candidate in the year immediately following a job change. Another marker is the proportion of subordinates who follow the candidate from job to job or task to task. If this characteristic is associated with success, it is normally a mark of the candidate's holding the loyalty of high-performing subordinates. Implicit in all the above characteristics, there must inevitably also be a very high energy level and a very high work rate, both of which will be apparent from the list of achievements in the candidate's track record. A high, persistent rate of target achievements in different environments is, of course, a strong indicator of these characteristics.

The last necessity for a good rescue specialist is a high level of stress tolerance. Indeed, it is almost necessary that the candidate enjoy a certain level of stress well above the comfort level for the general population. Research in the last 20 years means that it is now reasonably possible to estimate the level of stress at which the average man or woman will have a nervous breakdown. This prediction is made by adding up the number of 'stress points' a subject incurs in any six-month period of his life. There are ratings for a variety of high-stress occurrences such as bereavement, divorce, change of job, change of house, major change of income, birth of a child, and so forth. The scale normally used is standardised so that a total number of points of more than 500 in any six-month period tends to imply a high risk of nervous breakdown for the average person. Although it has made its way into pop psychology, the original work for this was carried out by the US Navy and was well validated. Although 500 points is the average, some people can clearly tolerate much higher levels. It is such a person one is seeking as a rescue specialist. Again, stress tolerance is quite difficult to measure. Yet there is a clue. People who have high stress tolerance typically do not enjoy lifestyles with much lower levels of stress and indeed are as uncomfortable under such circumstances as more normal people are at very high stress levels. The clue, therefore, is to look through the candidates record; if it appears that he is continually under pressure, continually facing new challenges, and indeed continually seeking new challenges perhaps both in his work and in his outside activities, then he is likely to be the character required. As a part of this measure we are also looking for a high level of determination. This test is self-evident, but it is a necessity frequently overlooked. Fortunately, anybody who has passed through all the other hoops is probably likely to have a sufficiently high level of determination.

Selection method

The interview procedure is the least effective method of finding a new chief executive for a company in need of rescue. Many of the attributes described already fit neatly into the self-image of a large number of people, but they bear no resemblance to reality at all. The best test of a person's ability to complete the rescue task is first his track record. Next come his references, then direct questioning of his acquaintances to see if he fits the criteria outlined above; and finally the interview.

Like the interview, references can be suspect. Obviously, no candidate will provide referees who are remotely likely to be uncomplimentary. It is therefore essential that all references are confirmed. This is best done by the interviewer in discussion directly with the referree using the seniority and extreme importance of the appointment as the reason for the detailed follow-up. In this way, some of the specific requirements of the job can be directly related to the known experience of the candidate.

The value of the interview is enhanced if it is directed specifically at testing whether many of these criteria are met, most particularly the technical knowledge and experience criteria. Some rescue specialists, most notably Michael Edwardes, put much emphasis on psychological testing. On the basis of evidence to date one cannot judge whether this is a valid method of assessment. It is, however, unlikely to give a better outcome than a thorough application of all the repertoire of information-gathering methods outlined in this section. Above all, however, *do not trust the interview alone.*

CHAPTER 5

Leadership in company rescues

■

In a typical rescue situation the key decision is the change of leader.[23] From this one decision virtually all others flow. The new leadership, in its widest sense, affects everybody who might influence the future of the troubled company. Perceptions of the new leadership will influence decisions by creditors and bankers, suppliers and customers, any of whom could choose to encourage or terminate the company. The workforce and management are likely to be in a state of either apathy or fear. Apathy dominates if a long history of failure has been accompanied by notions that 'this job is impossible', 'nobody could work harder', and 'we're bound to lose, so why try?' Alternatively, the organisation is likely shocked and paralysed by fear in the immediate realisation of the risks the company faces, and with them the possible loss of jobs of everybody who works for the company.

So leadership is key. Indeed, leadership may be *the* key to the survival of this company. And yet leadership is one of the most neglected subjects in management. When aspects of it are not neglected, they are prone to being fashionable. A fashion for participation and consultation – in themselves important parts of leadership – were carried to silly extremes in debates of the 1970s. The saddest example was the installation of worker directors in nationalised industries; rejected by their unions and mistrusted by their colleagues, they ended up as neither workers nor directors. Incentive systems, another important part of the leader's repertoire, have also been carried to foolish levels of complexity and subtlety.

The more recent wave of empirically and anecdotally based management literature has inevitably touched upon what makes a successful leadership style. Much of what is described in the Peters and Waterman 'excellence' books is a fundamental part of effective leadership: enthusiasm, value systems, 'loose/tight controls', all are aspects of the leadership side of management. More directly, John Kotter's study of general managers, already referred to, inevitably impinged on many aspects of effective leadership, and it identified some of the intuitive subtleties that differentiate the leadership styles of the most effective managers from all the rest.

What is certain is that leadership is much a more complex process than is acknowledged by most management theorists. What is also true is that leadership is about actions, and to a large extent many of these actions can be taught. This is not a new discovery. It was demonstrated by the British War Office nearly 50 years ago and described by John Adair, who wrote another seminal work on the subject.[24]

Rather than attempt to address the whole issue of leadership, this chapter will simply try to give the flavour of leadership style on that most testing of grounds, the company rescue.

Leadership style

The personal style of the leader of the rescue attempt will have influence beyond that exercised by most managers in most of their career. Leadership style is an extraordinary powerful technique.[25] But it is not a desiccated impersonal technique in any sense. This will be recognised immediately as it is about emotions, about value systems, and about symbols. Peoples' perceptions of it will be couched in words like care, and courage, and quality or, possibly, callousness, ruthlessness and cruelty. Few people's decisions and indeed few people's lives are in quite the same fish bowl as that in which the new chief executive finds himself. Personal behaviour will matter as much as personal directives. So, what guidelines exist to direct the new leader's behaviour? The following comments give a few ideas to communicate the flavour of the rules by which the new man has to live.

WORST FIRST

One simple guideline to sharply increase the new chief executive's effectiveness is to do the worst things first. In rescues there is always a brutal decision to be taken. It may be the closure of a factory or depot; it may be the firing of a senior colleague; it may be a difficult discipline case. The rule is to the deed quickly, indeed as soon as possible. This is true on the large time scale, when the toughest decisions should be implemented as soon as possible after the new chief executive arrives. it is also true on the more mundane, shorter daily time scale when the worst decisions should be implemented as soon as possible after they are taken. There are two reasons for this.

Firstly, even the sternest of leaders are only human, and so if not taken or not implemented a decision with unpleasant consequences preys on the mind and renders one ineffective until it is actually carried out. This alone is a good enough reason to do the worst things quickly.

Secondly, every chief executive in this circumstance must have some steel in his character, and that steel must be visible. The only way to make it visible is for the chief executive to show his willingness to take difficult decisions without hesitation. Suppliers, bankers, creditors, colleagues, employees and trade unions will all in their own ways respond healthily to such a characteristic.

Finally, a note of caution on this issue: never let this rule lead you to doing somebody an injustice. Abide by this, and it will not be difficult to win the trust of your people, and this is vital. Remember, a leader who lacks trust is lost.

WALK THE JOB

'Walking the job' is the process wherein the chief executive and indeed any other manager, goes out into the place of work of his various employees to speak to them and see what they are doing. This is a crucially important way for the chief executive to make himself visible. It is a highly effective way of getting across the values and value systems that underpin his strategy. And it is a superb way of gathering information.

As an example, it was possible to measure the success of 'walking the job' when I ran a recovery exercise on a transport company. The company had 30 locations, and in my monthly tour of a number of them, I had to take with me a notepad to keep a tally of all the points raised. At the end of the five-day tour, I typically had eighty follow-up items that required some sort of action. The number never dropped below fifty and occasionally reached into the high nineties. I learned more from talking to the warehousemen, the drivers, the forklift truck drivers, the clerks, the supervisors and the depot managers in a typical five-day tour than I could have done in a month of staff briefings. What is more, I got attention from all levels of management for issues that would otherwise have been ignored, and increased the responsiveness of that management to the operating problems of their own company.

The most difficult aspect of 'walking the job' is making time for it. In the midst of the hundreds of actions to be undertaken in that rescue,

I had to put aside five days every month to visit depots. It was done rigorously, it was never cancelled, and with hindsight it was all time well spent. This is easier in a factory or head office, but whatever the circumstance it should always be undertaken.

LEAD BY EXAMPLE

Because every move the chief executive makes in a rescue situation is watched incredibly closely, and is the common matter of discussion in the staff canteen and over the coffee machine, the chief executive has no choice but to lead by example. All he can choose is what sort of example he will set. If he chooses to visit customers regularly, his organisation will take customers seriously. If he is rigorous about deadlines, that will be reflected too. If he insists on 'right first time', his managers will emulate him. If he is assiduous about respecting lines of command and not undermining his managers, and about showing them respect, he will find others in the organisation showing them respect too. If nevertheless he does not worry about the non-functional aspects of status and hierarchy, and avoids the demeaning procedures that slip into too many hierarchical systems, his organisation will become more relaxed. If he is punctual and insists on punctuality in others, the foremans' team meetings will reflect it, and so will the board meetings. If he turns up on a night shift occasionally, or at six in the morning when the transport department becomes operational, those employees will feel more important and will very likely see more of their other managers too. If he gets to work first in the morning, he is likely to find his commitment to the job reflected even in the lowliest clerk and unskilled worker.

All these are good examples, of course. One could equally well cite the bad examples that presaged the decline of the British shipbuilding industry when managers turned up for work at ten in the morning, or the idleness and wasteful expenditure that dominated much of the management of Fleet Street and thereby legitimised the grotesque labour practices of that industry.

Finally, be warned of one thing. Many people think of leadership solely in terms of setting an example. That is wrong. Example alone will not actually make anything happen. It is only one part of the leader's repertoire.

PROMOTE PERFORMANCE

One direct aspect of leadership by example is the values that the chief executive applies when dealing with people. People will want to know what the new boss wants. If he promotes enthusiasm, ideas, and performance, the organisation will reflect it. One of the characteristics of successful turnarounds is that in them the management try to do more than in the unsuccessful ones. So the chief executive needs lots of new ideas. Indeed, because new ideas have a high failure rate, he needs hundreds of new ideas to generate dozens of actions.

This is the route to winning a recovery. The new chief executive must encourage enthusiasm, reward ideas, and most particularly reward performance. He must deliberately design what he says and does to support the doers in the organisation. He should promote performance in a number of ways: in the annual pay round, or in bonuses; with praise directly to the employee's peers or in the company newspaper; through promotion (in any turnaround there is a high management turnover and much scope for promotion); and by patronage, visiting departments and talking to employees, and always with the aim to support the achievers. Elsewhere we have discussed that the strategic and tactical need is for high productivity, high value added, but low capital expenditure. One must make the most of what one has with the maximum number of no-cost, low-cost changes. The new leader has the power to create exactly the right environment, to unleash the potential of his workforce, if he enforces precisely the right value system.

THE GIFT OF TIME

When groups of managers are asked to identify the most disruptive influence in their working life, usually they respond 'the boss'. The boss is unpredictable, impossible to ignore, and time consuming. This is a real paradox. It is no good being a first-class leader in everything you do if in doing so you take all the time of your subordinates and prevent them, in turn, being first-class leaders. The paradox is that the chief executive can exercise his power only through his managers.

The trick is to limit the discursive style of discussion, although effective, to meetings of simply one or two people. The more formal meetings of, say, half a dozen people should be concise, workmanlike, and relatively infrequent. In fact, the chief executive should issue a directive specifying to all departments of the organisation how these meetings should be run. For example, at least in the recovery stage of the rescue, and probably in perpetuity, a monthly performance review meeting is necessary. When going into a company the new chief executive may use this to shock the system into realising what is required of it. Typically, the chief executive issues a memo that is something like the following:

1. Meetings can be great wasters of time. They will be kept to a minimum.
2. In order to minimise the waste of time, the minimum number of people possible will come to each meeting.
3. To make use of the time effectively, all meetings will have proper agendas and the agenda will be circulated at least 24 hours in advance.
4. The agenda will identify which items require decision, which are for information, and who is to speak on each item.
5. An estimate as to the amount of time for the discussion on a given subject will be listed on the agenda. This is a guideline only, but ten minutes should not be interpreted to mean one hour.
6. No meeting should be planned to last more than one hour. No meeting that I chair will be allowed in practice to last more than one and a half hours.
7. The minutes of the meeting will simply list decisions taken, who is to implement them (at the lowest possible rank) and the date for implementation.
8. Those minutes will be circulated within 48 hours of completion of the meeting.
9. Lack of punctuality at meetings is not just discourteous, it is a gross waste of time. I will be punctual; so will you.
10. There will be no smoking at any meeting that I attend.

This format should be adhered to for any regular meeting. Generally speaking the meetings should be brisk and virtually always completed by the one and a half hour timetable or, though rarely, within one hour. Summary papers should always be required with the agenda and never allowed to be more than two pages long – other than the management accounts, which of course are in more detail. The minutes, really simply an action list, should be copied into an operations diary. In my own case, my secretary administered this. Each day she would telephone the person responsible for actions due for completion in the following day or two. This would warn them that I might well be checking up on them in the following day. Therefore no one was unnecessarily embarrassed, but no one was left in any doubt that a task allocated had better be a task completed.

Properly administered, such a system does a number of things:

1. It actually frees time for people to behave in a more discursive manner as described by Kotter, and certainly allows and encourages them to undertake the leadership actions described here and in following sections.
2. It symbolises clearly that time is the most precious commodity and that it should be used carefully.
3. It reinforces the commitment to using data in a digestible format.
4. It encourages a no-nonsense approach to solving problems.
5. It drives all the way down through the organisation an unremitting and uncompromising commitment to action and results.

Each of the meetings should start with a review of actions not completed but due in the last month. This should be a short part of the meeting, necessary only while people get used to the follow-up system. This occasionally may be the most uncomfortable part of the meeting, but in very short order it will make the point and within six months it should become a completely redundant exercise. It should be an agenda with no entries!

CHALLENGE EVERYTHING, FOLLOW UP EVERYTHING

Companies in trouble are invariably rife with rumour. Unless the new leader insists on factual support for argument, he and his management team will soon find themselves chasing their tail about problems that do not exist while ignoring the problems that invariably do exist. Thus the habit of challenging everything that might be an assertion is a good one to encourage.

Some things, however, cannot be measured. New ideas in particular would wither under a regime that demanded that everything be proved. And so the habits of experiments, tests and trials should be encouraged. Thus small quantities of factory time, money, sales force effort, should be given over to trying out new products, new processes, new methods. This should be a way of encouraging youngsters. It should be managerial seedcorn – small investment, high wastage, but potentially enormous in yield.

POWER OF THE PARABLE

The new leadership must bring with it new values, new aims and of course new levels of commitment. Clearly this has to be communicated throughout the company. To be effective this message must be understandable by everybody within the company, not just by the senior management. It has to be in manageable and concrete terms for the people who carry out their jobs to be able to turn it into reality on the shop floor and in front of the customer. The message must also be simple. The easiest way to simplify is to use parables or anecdotes, stories of how greater quality is achieved, greater reliability managed, lower costs implemented; stories that demonstrate the principle in concrete action. Over time these parables are transmitted and new ones are created and become part of the corporate folklore. As such they are more powerful than any manual, standard operating procedure or system of discipline. The entire workforce of the company comes to realise that every day they are fighting an election in which the votes are cast by the customers and counted by the bankers – an election they must not lose.

Disseminating leadership

In an organisation of any size, however, for leadership to be effective it must be practiced by all levels of management. This is frequently overlooked by turnaround specialists, and it is one reason why companies sink back into the morass after the specialist has moved on.

Leadership is one of the least well taught aspects of management. Yet it is not necessarily innate and can be taught straightforwardly. Indeed, many institutions, military and commercial, have been teaching leadership successfully for a long time. The best-established and still possibly the most effective method of teaching leadership is that originally described by John Adair and used today by many organisations, most notably the Industrial Society.[26] This method is symbolised in Fig. 5.1, showing the inter-relationship of the three components of leadership, namely achieving the task, building the team, and developing the individual.

TASK

In any organisation with a purpose, achieving that purpose, the organisation's task, takes precedence over the other two components of leadership, namely maintenance of the team and support of the individuals. Were that not true armies would never fight battles, companies would never manufacture anything, and indeed very little would be done. In a company rescue, the task is if anything even more important. Thus the first element for a rescue leader in pursuit of the

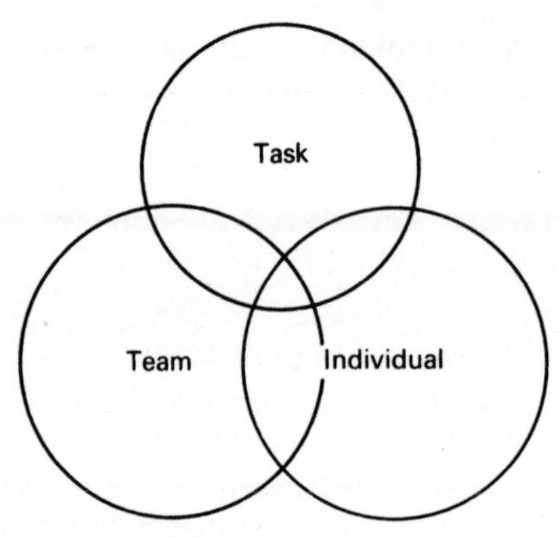

Source: The Industrial Society.

Fig. 5.1. Inter-relationship of the three components of leadership.

company's task is to describe that task in clear concrete objectives. He should make the task simple and incremental rather than complex and long term. In particular he should avoid big gambles and periods of time too long to measure, especially in the early stages of a rescue attempt.

Towards this end he should design the task of his subordinates to encourage the commitment of individuals. The jobs should be achievable within a finite period of time so that they are in bite-size chunks. They should be designed to fit in clearly with others, and that fit should be defined so that each person understands his interdependence with the rest of the team. This will not only make the task easier to achieve but will reinforce team cohesion. The job should be so described to enable measurement of success or failure. And that measurement should also be carried out, for 'What gets measured gets done'.

Communicating an understanding of a how all the tasks fit company aims is important. Managers and team leaders should get into the habit of asking their subordinates 'What have we done today that has helped: the team, the company or our customers?' Clear accountability should be established. The simple task for accountability is 'Whom do I report to when my task is complete? Who is responsible for checking the quality of my task? Who tells me what my next task is?' With that accountability should go the habit of measuring progress.

The leader should set standards of achievement and should understand that sometimes to get reasonable results you have to take unreasonable stances. A very common characteristic of failing companies is that the entire staff feel they are working flat out and that therefore nothing else can be done. Clearly, if this is really true then the company is dead. However, for those jobs not limited by hardware (such as assembly line work), it is a good general rule to say that in a rescue individuals can achieve two to three times their previous useful output. Quite often this comes from working smarter rather than working harder, but it means that managers in a rescue situation are always asking people to do things that the conventional wisdom says is impossible: 'This plant cannot handle that output', 'that customer would never pay that price', 'that supplier could never manage that quality', and 'we could never get the union to accept that'. This does not mean that the company in turnaround is like a latter-day Rourke's Drift. It is simply that with changes in method must go changes in expectations. Managers must learn to be unreasonable with a smile.

The managers also must make sure they do a very careful job of planning the physical and task environment. After all, the managers' fundamental task is to plan how the job can be done, to define and provide the relevant resources and to ensure that the physical conditions are right. It is remarkable how frequently Western managers fall down dramatically on this job. For example, they tolerate filthy and untidy conditions, in which often it must be very difficult to think straight, let alone work effectively. The Japanese understand this better than anybody else. They know that a lick of paint and frequent applications of a broom can lead to an entire different attitude by the workforce, the supervisors and the management. Indeed, the first public sign of raising standards is when the chief executive explodes at the state of one of his factories. It is an important signal and a repetitive one, and one that should not be ignored because it appears to be trivial, for it is anything but trivial to the people who work in the factory or depot or office concerned.

Sloppiness often extends to an 'out of sight, out of mind' attitude to many of the physical support systems. Woodruff Imberman studied what actually caused strikes in US companies.[27] Part of his findings are summarised in Table 5.1, which shows a high correlation between strike-prone companies and those companies not paying attention to making sure that, for example, the maintenance systems and the maintenance stores worked properly on the night shift.

Such inattention to detail causes enormous frustration. And this frustration on the part of the workforce completely, and rightly, undermines their confidence in their management. An atmosphere of frustration rapidly becomes an atmosphere of failure: 'If the management don't try, why should we?' It is therefore the key job of management to remove the external limits upon what a member of the

Table 5.1. Complaints about third-shift working conditions

Complaint	16 strike plants	14 non-strike plants
Shortage of materials or tools	12 plants	4 plants
Shortage of maintenance personnel	14	3
Problems with foremen	14	4
No personnel representation	13	3
No visits from top executives	12	2

Source: Woodruff Imberman, 'Who strikes and why?', *Harvard Business Review* (Nov.-Dec. 1983).

company can achieve, so that left are only those limits the individual worker has put upon himself. If managers were to do this more frequently, they would discover that the self-imposed limits are broad indeed.

Managers who are careful to eliminate all the unnecessary physical constraints find that they can very easily fulfil their other task of pacing the work. Pace, or work rate, must inevitably increase in the course of the company rescue. More often than not failures to achieve increases in pace occur, not because of worker reticence, but because of lack of attention to the detail. Usually it is poor systems that limit what the worker can achieve.

INDIVIDUALS

Attention to the individual means maintaining a very high level of motivation. And for an individual, motivation means all the following:

1. A need to experience individual achievement.
2. A need to feel he is making worthwhile contributions.
3. The need to feel that the job is challenging.
4. The need to receive adequate recognition.
5. The need to have adequate control over the job.
6. Depending on the individual, the need to feel a degree of security in the job, and possibly that he is developing in the job.

To achieve this the leader must act as follows:

1. Set lists of short-term targets.
2. Ensure that the individuals have the resources necessary, including the authority and the skills, and fill any shortfall with proper training.

3. Undertake performance reviews, not just once a year, but on a smaller scale much more frequently.
4. Recognise success and indeed also recognise failure. This means giving a good deal of time and attention to individuals, something which is always difficult to a busy manager, but something which virtually always pays dividends.

It is essential to stress the importance of a person's job. A friend of mine tells a story of how, when on tour around a company, he asked a young girl what she did. She replied, 'Oh, I'm not important. I'm just the sales clerk'. The next ten minutes was spent asking the details of what she did, and pointing out to her the important role she filled in ensuring that the customers' orders were taken accurately, and fulfilled speedily and effectively. He pointed out how vital to the company's success it was that she was cheerful and helpful, and how important to the customer it was, if he had a problem, to be able to talk to somebody who was sympathetic and who could direct him to the correct source of help, even if she could not give the answers herself. The key message was 'Your job is important – indeed vital – and we depend on you to do it well'. When people understand this about their role, it almost always leads to an increase in both effort and quality of work.

The leader, however, must be intolerant of unnecessary failure. When people are lazy, or thoughtless, or plain sloppy, the damage they do must be made clear to them, and they must understand the consequences for them, their team and the whole company. If the leader is convinced that the person is trying but makes mistakes, then clearly an exercise in coaching is to be carried out. Here is a description of coaching from the chief executive of a medium-sized retail operation:

> The university word 'tutoring' is the best word to describe one of the most important social skills of a manager. He has to teach people on a close-up, man to man basis. I have seen it done superbly by one of my area managers, whenever he takes on a new branch manager. He sits in with him and goes around with him for hours at the beginning, talking over every aspect of the job and working alongside. Then he gradually lets go and the nature of the things referred to the area manager changes as the new man picks up the reins, making his own decisions on many things within the limits of the policies he has absorbed.[28]

Of course, that someone is not achieving may be due to personal factors and the individual may deserve counselling by the leader. Equally, there may be a need for short training for groups of underachievers.

Another characteristic is that the leader must not be exclusively one thing or the other; he must not either always praise or always scold. In short, it is the willingness to praise that gives the right to scold. And it is the perception of justice that creates the acceptance of authority. Yet discipline does not have to be formal. Reliance solely on formal discipline systems is often a sign of poor morale and poor team cohesion, again as demonstrated by Imberman's study (see Table 5.2).

Table 5.2. Number of grievances over a three-month period

Issue	28 strike plants	28 non-strike plants
Suspension	498 grievances	43 grievances
Seniority	189	39
Transfers	152	43
Terminations	125	37
Discipline warnings	124	29
Vacation	110	39
Other	87	36
Total	1285	266

Source: Woodruff Imberman, 'Who strikes and why?', *Harvard Business Review* (Nov.-Dec. 1983).

Delegation is often difficult in a company rescue, but at some stage in a recovery delegation will become necessary. One must remember to delegate and not to abdicate; to *maintain* minimum controls on key variables, but also to *limit* those controls to the minimum necessary. In this way one creates a great sense of autonomy and pride and normally obtains high performance. Systematic controls do not have to be formal controls, however. Further, as described earlier, a walk around the work area can teach as much as a thick report.

In addition, the leader should know the teams and design the jobs to make the best use of the skills they have. In the peculiar circumstances of company rescue a massive effort is needed, for the more strategies and tactics that management attempts in a rescue, the more that will succeed. The more that succeed, the more likely the company is to make a short-term recovery and to achieve long-term stability and growth. So we have to encourage our teams to make many attempts for a few successes. We have to reward visibly and frequently those small innovations and successes, and not once a year but many times. We should not penalise single failures, but we should keep a tally of who succeeds because tomorrow's leaders should be coming from today's shop floor innovators. In looking for tomorrow's leaders we should look not first for intelligence, as is normal in most management groups, but for determination. Given the choice between determination and intelligence, always choose the former over the latter. And we should let our people know that they earn their authority and they earn their power: success earns the right to play again, with bigger stakes.

Finally, with respect to individuals, we must teach our leaders the virtues of speedy follow-up. One piece of wisdom discovered by Woodruff Imberman in his study of strikes was that speed mattered more than anything else in dealing with grievances and personal problems. A very high correlation existed between the incidence of strikes and the slowness of grievance procedures (see Table 5.3). Detailed follow-up demonstrated that when there was a grievance it was better to give a quick, tough answer than a slow, soft one. Grievances almost always occur in company rescues, as jobs are changed, more things are expected and, quite often, less is given. Deal with these grievances quickly even if the answer is a plain no. Then they do not fester and the management keeps the respect of its workforce. This advice is difficult to follow, but followed it must be.

Table 5.3. Time required for grievance settlement

Stage of grievance filing	28 strike plants	28 non-strike plants
First step	3.7 days	1.9 days
Second step	12.9	4.6
Third step	38.5	15.1
Arbitration	126.5	46.0

Source: Woodruff Imberman, 'Who strikes and why?', *Harvard Business Review* (Nov.-Dec. 1983).

TEAM

Many of the points made about individuals apply to team maintenance as well. However, maintaining the unity of the team is helped by a number of actions in addition to those we apply to individuals. Firstly, we should get the size of the team right, preferably between 3 and 12 people, but certainly not more than 15 people for one team leader to run. The more complex the task, the smaller the team. We should build teamwork into jobs, make the interdependence clear cut and discuss it whenever necessary. Always act promptly on disruptive influences, be they individuals, or uneven work or pay or overtime.

Managers often talk about communication. It is a key issue to team unity, and in a fast-changing and stressful environment of a company rescue it is vital. The 'team briefing' approach taught by the Industrial Society in Britain and a number of other Commonwealth countries is an excellent means of communicating. It is simple, it is systematic, and it does not depend upon any great genius to carry it out. It also works. The approach hinges on regular meetings of teams, meetings which are kept short and concentrate on the four areas of people, progress, policy and points for action. These single-direction meetings are never allowed to become negotiating forums or indeed even consultation forums. There are other meetings for that. As such the 'team briefing' is clean, clear cut, and effective.

Leaders should give a lot and expect a lot from their teams. They should do this not just for effort, but for thought. In a turnaround we need a firestorm of ideas, and to achieve this we should encourage experiment. Each team should be able to obtain small allocations of resources and money to try out new ideas. The policy of small commitments, quick cuts of failures, and strong support for winners should be made explicit and publicised. A habit of 'don't debate it, try it' should be encouraged. We should encourage the habit of competitive plagiarism, namely teaching teams to keep their eyes open for other people's best ideas, whether those other people be competitors, other industries, suppliers, or indeed customers. And where there are successes we should reward the whole team.

With the most knotty problems, leaders should consider using what the Americans call 'Tiger Teams'. These consist of special groups of people of different disciplines including, for example, an engineer, an accountant, a marketing representative and those with any other skills necessary to the achievement of the required solution. The teams must have a properly accountable leader. Again, these teams should be set extraordinarily high targets to be achieved within a very short time. Experience shows that they usually succeed.

Other personnel issues

Other issues to consider in the rescue operation are training programs, incentive schemes, and the complexity of the company's organisation. These issues are considered next.

TRAINING

Not enough money is spent on training; too much money is wasted on training. Paradoxically, these statements are true in most companies. Training is one way that companies can achieve a sustainable competitive edge. It does not occur in the public domain and is difficult to imitate. The problem is that for that very reason people waste money on it. Training should be undertaken in a clinical manner, specifically tailored for the individual's present or future job. Before training is undertaken, one should determine exactly what outcome is expected. Is it better leadership? If so, how does one measure that? Is it better technical skills? If so, what will be trainee be able to achieve at the end of the programme? The training should be chosen and tailored rigorously on the basis of what is expected, and when the trainees return from training they should have an action plan to complete that they would not have been able to achieve without the training. These practical guidelines can save companies from wasting a great deal of money and radically enhance the effectiveness of training. *Cheap, practical, effective* and *frequent* should be the watchwords of the training policy. For these reasons, training should be authorised and monitored by line managers, not personnel staff. In the months after training the questions 'what did they teach you to do?' and 'have you done it?' should be regularly asked by the employees' managers.

INCENTIVE SCHEMES

There is very strong evidence indeed that incentive schemes work particularly well under circumstances of underperforming companies. In addition to all of the academic evidence that exists, the whole management buy-out movement of the last few years is based upon the presumption that success can be attained by the same management, but with much enhanced financial motivation. There are, however, some rigorous guidelines to creating an effective incentive scheme. Fortunately they are simple. Successful incentive schemes are characterised as follows:

1. They are large in their impact on the employee's salary (at least 20%).
2. They show quick returns on effort (i.e. not yearly or multi-year).
3. They go to a relatively low level in the organisation.
4. They are simple.
5. They bear a direct relationship to the job and aspects of the job that are controllable by the employee.

Break these rules and you risk wasting your money with an incentive scheme.

ORGANISATION

Probably very few organisations indeed, if any, need more than five or six levels of organisation. With a span of command of between four and twelve, this gives the range of maximum company size from over a thousand to over a million depending on task complexity. Anything larger than this is liable to lead to an organisation with no responsiveness at all. Since one of the great causes of company failure is losing touch with its market place and its basic business, this is clearly something to avoid. In practice, four or five levels is normally enough.

'Dotted-line responsibilities' are also to be avoided. Any degree of ambiguity or vagueness about who is responsible for what is liable to make the organisation less responsive. Who should respond to what problem should always be clear. Although many of the fancy organisational structures mooted in the last decade may have valuable advantages under some circumstances, the middle of a company rescue is not a time to experiment with organisational innovation. The well-proven methods are what we have to choose.

This noted, we should not miss out on the qualitative ideas for improving the responsiveness of the organisation. Clearly it is valuable to concentrate the information and power at the lowest possible level to improve the speed and quality of decision making, particularly in production and marketing. We should also actively seek ways of improving the communications between the organisation's different departments and between each of those departments and the customers, suppliers and other outsiders upon whom they depend. Nothing in conventional organisations prevents sales managers doing a short tour of duty in the distribution section or on the factory floor to improve their understanding of how their product works.

Similarly, supervisors and blue-collar workers should visit customers, if appropriate. The best example to demonstrate the effectiveness of this occurred when we sent an elderly supervisor in a starch plant to visit a customer who used the product that the supervisor was responsible for manufacturing. Walking around the customer's premises, the supervisor suddenly realised that his product was used in manufacturing the baby food that his own granddaughter ate. From that point forward it was never again necessary to reinforce the importance of quality to either that supervisor or his team or any of the teams with whom he had any contact.

Leadership matters. Leadership works. Once the new chief executive has decided what the task is, it should be his priority to decide what his leadership actions will be to achieve it.

CHAPTER 6

Negotiation

■

There are two categories of negotiation that the new chief executive must consider in great detail before he arrives in a target company. First are obviously those negotiations he has to complete before taking up the reins, and second are those negotiations so important that he must shape the conditions under which they occur. In the first category typically are negotiations with financial institutions and occasionally creditors. In the second category normally are suppliers, trade unions and occasionally customers.

This book is not the place to review the whole technique of negotiation, for which there exist a number of more comprehensive books. However, in outline it is worth considering the structure in which one addresses the problems of negotiations.

The other side

Adequate preparation for negotiation is vital. The first essential step is to view your problem from the perspective of the other side. For each group you should study their needs and objectives, their expectations and their options. These areas are not always as clear cut as one might expect. For example, the needs and objectives of any bank usually include protecting the interests of its investors and making the maximum possible return for them. However, a local bank manager may extend a loan to avoid taking a significant write-off in his branch or his loan portfolio in a particular year. Accordingly, he may be more willing to co-operate in any rescue attempt than one would normally expect. Similarly, a trade union normally puts the preservation of its members' jobs ahead of all else. However, occasions do occur when other issues transcend this consideration. For example, battles over membership with other unions can sometimes sharpen this objective and at other times can appear to neutralise it. One must be aware of this possibility so that the trade union's *apparently* irrational or unpredictable behaviour does not cripple a constructive negotiation.

With suppliers one assumes the aim is to get the largest contract with the highest price. If the target company is a major customer of theirs, perhaps even responsible for more than half their business, this may not be quite the first concern. Their principal concern may indeed be the same as our own, namely to keep the target company in business. It may also be possible for them to enhance their profitability in ways that do not involve a higher price but that are to our advantage – cutting the quantity of rejects, for example.

The point of each of these examples is simply to demonstrate that the opening negotiating position may not be as simple as appears at first sight. Understanding clearly the intent of the other side is the first step to a mutually successful negotiation and quite often turns a straight win or lose style of negotiation into something more creative and mutually beneficial.

The second issue, that of the other side's expectations, can be equally vague. They may be acutely conscious of the difficulties the company is in and very afraid it is going bankrupt. In the case of trade unions, they may simply not believe that the situation is as bad as it has been described and may view the whole approach as a negotiating gambit by management. Suppliers, on the other hand, may be panicking in the other direction, particularly if a poor financial department and poor controls have led to frequent non-payment of bills. The new chief executive must decide which of these expectations and understandings are worth changing in the interest of the target company.

The third thing we should discover is what the various players see as their options. Is the trade union likely to see a strike as an appropriate response to a workforce reduction programme? Does the bank think that if it forces a liquidation now it will be able to recover all its assets and accrued interest from the sale of the assets of the company? Do our customers consider they can go easily to another supplier, and will they get an equally good price and quality deal after one of the competitors has disappeared from the business? Do our suppliers consider us an unimportant part of their sales programme, and those of them that are creditors consider their best option is to sue for bankruptcy? Once these have been considered, it is worth deciding how we can set about changing some of these views.

Our needs

The next consideration is to identify our own needs. It is most important to draw up a comprehensive shopping list. A good deal of thought should go into this, since we wish at this stage to establish the following:

1. All our likely requirements.
2. Some margin for error (since at this stage we do not have full information).
3. Some negotiating margin (which we would prefer to keep but can afford to lose in the course of discussions).

It is quite normal to feel that the list of demands seems enormous and that it is inconceivable that the stakeholders and various people involved will accept it. This concern should be ignored, since at this stage everybody has a lot to lose. That can concentrate minds wonderfully. What we must determine is, what actions by the other stakeholders do we want to avoid at all costs? This is the risk analysis part of the negotiation. Can we afford a strike? For the whole of the business or part of the business? Can we afford to lose the support of our bankers? Could the support be replaced? Can we afford to lose a proportion of our customers? Which ones? Having considered these risks it is possible to determine which ones we are incapable of withstanding. Inevitably at this juncture some gambles will have to be taken, but at least now are possible clear priorities as to which risks to avoid. It is also possible at this point to determine what price we think can be paid. Are we willing to close and liquidate part of the business to appease some of the stakeholders? Are we willing to accept closure of parts of the business in response to a strike? The detail will be specific to the individual company.

Strategy and tactics

We will then have to determine the negotiating strategy. The first part of the strategy will inevitably be a perception-shaping exercise. Some of it will be explicit and often factual. For example, if the assets of the company are unlikely to realise much on liquidation, it is worth letting the bank and the creditors know to prevent their precipitating an unnecessary and useless bankruptcy. If at this stage we have not taken on the rescue attempt, it may also be worthwhile making a degree of co-operation a contractual condition of taking it on. Much of the perception-shaping exercise, however, will be implicit in behaviour with the various stakeholders. Typically the exercise will work as detailed in the sections that follow.

WELL THOUGHT THROUGH PLANS

Clear plans of action with timetables are always great confidence builders, particularly for creditors. If creditors can see a possibility of a return without a distasteful and unpleasant legal action, they are much more likely to give support than they otherwise might. The key issues here are confidence, clarity and detailed information as it applies to the particular stakeholder's interest. Even trade unions react much more positively when they face a manager with a clear vision of where he wants to go, and why, even if they do not particularly like the consequences for their own membership.

ACTIONS PRIOR TO START OF NEGOTIATIONS

These actions can do a great deal to build confidence and respect. Liquidation, prompt sales of unnecessary assets and payment of bills on time, or at least to a predictable timetable, have a remarkable effect upon the attitudes of creditors. Similarly, if closures and lay-offs *have* to be carried out, better do them sooner rather than later. This is a repetitive theme of this book, but it cannot be said too many times. Trade union leaders are less likely to call the bluff of someone who has already shown his determination to carry through a cost reduction programme than they are if he has not. Accordingly, doing the toughest things first can in the end reduce the total number of jobs lost by avoiding the risk of negotiations poorly judged by the unions.

Finally, a general air of visible determination and activity is extremely important to the perception-shaping exercise. It is remarkable how qualitative judgements of character feature large in the way people respond to a company in trouble.

Having determined the positions of the various stakeholders, the negotiator can put together the offer and, very importantly, its rationale. A wider repertoire of possible ways of approaching the negotiation exist, but these can be studied at length in the specialist books on negotiation.[29] Nevertheless, a few common denominators apply.

The negotiation meetings

Assuming the preparatory work has been done, and we have a view of the costs to each party of agreement, deadlock, and disagreement, it is worth making explicit decisions on who negotiates, where the negotations take place, and what concession pattern should be used.

WHO NEGOTIATES?

The determination of who negotiates may be made for us, but generally we can decide ourselves. If possible the decision maker should avoid being the negotiator; separation of these functions allows flexibility of response, encourages explicit tactical planning, and allows a 'court of appeal' in case of deadlock. It gives better returns for lower risk. The exceptions tend to occur when the decision maker's presence adds something vital – confidence in dealing with bankers and creditors; finality with unions; an implied high priority and 'special' attention for customers.

WHERE?

Negotiations should take place on home ground, if possible. We all negotiate better when we are in familiar surroundings, and we can design them to favour our own position. It is also possible to shape perceptions better – by showing the bankers the new cost reduction exercise in action, or the customer the quality-checking procedures.

WHAT CONCESSION PATTERN?

Experimental and empirical evidence support the following statements:

1. Buyers who start with low offers do better.
2. Buyers who give a large amount in one concession raise buyer expectation.
3. Sellers who are willing to take less, get less.
4. People who give a little at a time do better.
5. Losers made the first concession on major issues.
6. Deadlines forced decisions and agreements.
7. Quick negotiations were very bad for one party or the other.
8. People who make the largest single concession do poorly.[30]

The evidence thus tends to support a tactical plan that says 'start tough, organise so as to negotiate to a deadline that suits ourselves, do not make the first major concession, make piecemeal concessions with a declining concession pattern and keep all concessions low. Make the opposition work for their concessions, and when the deal is struck make them feel that they have done well. Remember, they may have to sell the idea to someone else in their own organisation!'

What should not be forgotten throughout the exercise, however, is that the risk for everybody involved is very large, and this puts a massive premium on nerve. He who has least to lose always has the upper hand in these circumstances. If the exercise is properly entered into from the beginning, that initiative should always stay with the rescuer.

CHAPTER 7

Analysis and action

■

What has to be achieved in the rescue is highlighted well by Fig. 7.1, which summarises data from a study by Schendel and Patton of US turnarounds.[31] Large increases in cash flow and profit were generated in the study sample on the back of sharp increases in sales and margins. Sales increased on every measure, be it sales per employee, sales per dollar of capital employed or sales per item of equipment. Margins increased partly as a result of a reduction in cost of goods sold, but also markedly from other factors, including presumably price increases, product mix improvements and programmes of enhanced value to the customer. Inventory turnover was radically increased, which had marked effects on cash flow, and of course reduced cost of goods sold. This would have had a notable effect directly upon profits and indirectly upon the ability to compete.

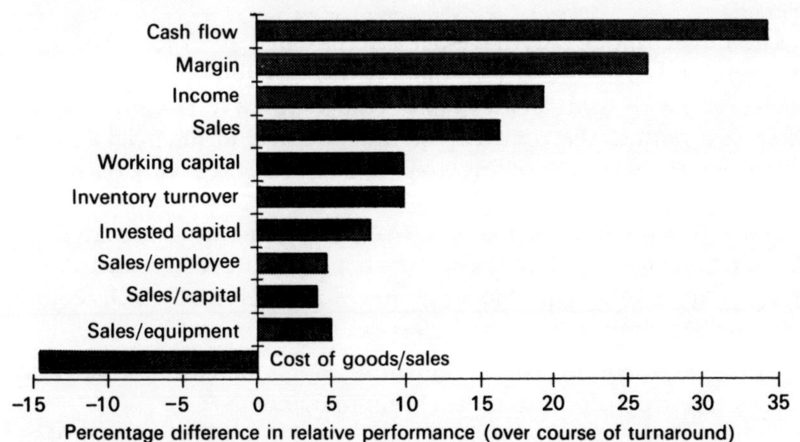

Source: Based upon Dan E. Schendel and G. R. Patton, 'Corporate stagnation and turnaround', *Journal of Economics and Business*, vol. 28, pp. 236–41.

Fig. 7.1. Performance of turnaround companies versus non-turnaround companies.

Analysis

In determining the outline action plan for the rescue, it is necessary to do the following:

1. Assess the causes of decline.
2. Determine the target goal.
3. Decide on the general strategy.

At this stage the causes of decline should already have been determined. If the causes are strategic, either because of changes in industry structure or because of poor strategic decision making by previous management, then the course of the rescue will be dictated also by the industry structure. Undoubtedly, complex industries, with large amounts of 'texture' in their market structure and highly differentiable products, improve the chances of rescue enormously. Niche marketing is at once a very effective defensive and offensive weapon.

If the causes of decline are operational, the focus of the rescue will tend to be on the implementation aspects. In general operational declines are reversible. While the original cause will direct the focus of the rescue plan, always remember that strategic targets require operational implementation, and operational recoveries have to take place within their industrial context. It is important not to forget one aspect whilst concentrating on the other. Further, turnarounds fail more often from poor execution than poor strategy; implementation is crucial.

The target will already have been determined as either recovery or recovery and sale. This determination will dictate both timetable and tactics. Recovery and sale normally requires just a tidying-up exercise, often just putting the company on an even keel in financial and cost terms. For the purposes of this chapter, a full-scale recovery is assumed to be the target.

Once the causes of decline have been determined and the target set, the decision on general strategy can be made. Whatever the thrust of the strategy, it is likely to have at least three phases, each of which requires different techniques. These three phases are as follows:

1. *Crisis management.* This is the survival-dominated phase in which the principal aim is to create room to manoeuvre.
2. *Consolidation and control.* This is essentially the continuation of the 'tough-minded' phase of the operation. This phase continues until the company and chief executive arrive at the first plateau on the learning curve, when the pace of change starts to slow down.

3. *Capitalising on success.* This phase is concerned with maintaining momentum and turning the 'dog' into a 'star'. This is the most difficult phase to manage because although crisis management flows naturally into consolidation, the methods involved in maintaining momentum involve a number of changes in management style.

   These changes in management style are an important part of understanding the whole process, and they apply to whatever area one is examining. Leadership in the early days relies at least to some extent upon fear, while as time goes on it should, if it is healthy, rely upon growing enthusiasm in success. In organisational terms the early phases will be marked by sharp centralisation of control as the new chief executive takes a grip of the organisation, but for reasons of both pyschology and effectiveness this would be reversed into a heavy decentralisation programme as the company achieves an even keel and starts to grow once more. The early phases are likely to be marked by a rationalisation of product lines, eliminating unnecessary and low-profit products, whereas the concentration of the later phases will be to add features and to add quality to the products. In the early stages price increases, and possibly even harvesting strategies, will dominate the thinking of the sales force; later, market share will be dominant. In manufacturing in the early stages cost reduction will probably dominate; in the later stages quality and output will be key. Managing this transition is not easy, and it need not necessarily be carried through by a single chief executive. There is nothing wrong with a rescue specialist carrying on until he can promote one of his best managers, or import another chief executive, to carry the growth phase.

Management changes

The action programme commences with the assumption that the company has a new chief executive. The new chief executive will question whether the second tier of management is capable of carrying through what will be a stressful and difficult programme. The first decision that has to be addressed is whether the company needs a new financial director or financial vice-president. It is highly probable that the company will need new control systems, and that the old systems have failed. There is, therefore, likely to be good cause for replacement. In addition, because of the easy transferability of accounting skills, replacing the head of finance is the lowest risk in management change that could be imposed.

For the others, risk of change is a key issue. It is difficult in a short while either to judge the competence of the main heads of department or indeed to determine the company's exact needs in those roles. Since any personnel replacement is a high-risk measure, it is probably advisable to work with the team in place for a short period at least. If nothing else, this will allow the new chief executive to assess whether any of the lower management tier are capable of being promoted into head-of-department jobs. Caution, therefore, is probably advisable in this area; occasions where such caution is inappropriate, and where there is a need for sharp change, will generally be very obvious.

Financial reorganisation

Financial reorganisation is the part of the operation that is entirely about creating room for manoeuvre. It may involve one or several of the following:

1. Taking major write-offs of assets (and equity).
2. Infusing new equity.
3. Restructuring the existing debt.
4. Introducing a new long-term lender.
5. Organising new creditor arrangements.

Although these options all look generally awful, in reality this is by no means always the case. Outside stakeholders in the company are frequently relieved to see the management take grip of a worrying problem and do something about it. When ARCO, the US oil company, took an enormous write-off in one year, its stock market price actually increased. Creditors and bankers are often keen to avoid recognising a bad debt or a defaulting loan, and for that reason they are more willing to look more kindly on such arrangements than a manager might imagine.

Control systems

The most frequent symptom of failing companies is that they have poor financial, information and other control systems. It is therefore of vital importance to install basic systems as quickly as possible. Key system requirements are these:

1. Cash flow forecasting, analysis and control systems.
2. Working capital summary analyses, including age analysis of

debtors and creditors, and if possible a turnover, use, and obsolescence analysis of inventories.

3. Cost control system.
4. Profit-margin analysis by product, and area or customer.

These are minimum requirements. Even these, however, will take some time to install, and once installed will not give immediate feedback. The new chief executive will undoubtedly look to quick, rough-and-ready measures, such as tonnage output, or numbers output, numbers of rejects, physical stock levels, head count, and daily cash balance at bank. These are merely illustrative, but they give the flavour of the sort of indicative measures that might be used while more thorough systems are being installed. At this point simplicity and speed take precedence over precision.

Table 7.1 gives an indication of the sort of timetables to which the control systems should operate. The table is illustrative only and as it stands is appropriate for an industrial goods company.

Table 7.2, a checklist on cost control systems, includes a number of points that are key to the effectiveness of the systems, most of them being obvious to anyone with a degree of common sense. For example, no system is effective unless it is reliable, accurate, and quick. The tendency for most accounting based systems is to try to fulfil the first two of these requirements to excess, and the last not at all. Speed is important. Rescue specialists do not have time to read history books. By the same measure the reports need to be brief, simple to read and relevant. Even more crucial, however, is that they discover the causes of the deviations identified, and that actions are taken to correct the problems identified. Finally, it is fundamentally important that a proper follow-up ensures that the actions are carried out on time and are successful. Quite often the bases of good control systems do exist within failing companies, but they are either too slow or not properly used. In these circumstances the quickest move is simply to change the organisation to make use of those systems that do exist.

Basic balance sheets, cash flow budgets, cost analyses, product costings and capital expenditure reports do not have to be complex or sophisticated at this stage. The proformas for these items can be taken straight out of any financial management textbook; illustrative examples are given throughout the chapter.

BALANCE SHEET

In the context of a rescue the basic balance sheet (shown in Table 7.3)

Table 7.1. Frequency of critical reports

Report	Prior to decision or daily	Weekly	Monthly	Quarterly or other
Sales				
Total company sales output	X			
New contracts, new bids	X			
Sales by convenient product *or* location *or* customer grouping		X		
Sales by major product *and* location *and* customer grouping			X	
Average sales prices by product group			X	
Contributions and net profit margins by major product line			X	
Worst-case margins, by product, customer or individual contract; contributions and net margin basis				X
Costs and profits				
Headcount, by department	X			
Discretionary expenses above trigger level	X		X	
Major cost categories		X	X	
Other costs			X	
Net profit			X	
Cash				
Bank balance	X			
Cash flow		X		
Debtors		X		
Inventory		X		
Capital expenditure			X	
General				
Financial/physical impact of agreed actions		X		

Source: Based on item in *Inc* (March 1981), p.76.

Table 7.2. Checklist on cost control

Effectiveness

1. Is the costing system reliable, accurate, and quick?
2. Are control reports brief, simple to read, and relevant?
3. Does information from the cost control system highlight the critical factors that govern the company's success in achieving its objectives?
4. Are control reports used to indicate relative efficiencies?
5. Are deviations reported rapidly?
6. Do controls help to explain variancies and to indicate the corrective action that is required?
7. Are actions taken on the basis of these reports?
8. Is there a follow-up system to ensure that the corrective action is undertaken?

Accountability

1. Do controls conform to the oranisational structure?
2. Is cost control information designed to meet the requirements of accountable individuals?
3. Are cost control requirements and reports discussed with recipients?
4. Do control reports cover both financial and related causal factors?
5. Do all employees understand the cost implications of their work?
6. Do all who require it receive cost information? At the lowest workable level?
7. Do those individuals responsible for various costs really have control over these costs?
8. Do recipients of control information know how to extract the most essential facts?
9. Are cost controls established according to the nature of the tasks?
10. Do all employees have cost targets (where relevant)?

Source: Derived from R. M. S. Wilson, *Cost Control Handbook*.

gives, essentially, indicative answers *only* to three questions, namely these:

1. What are the sources of the company's employed capital, and most particularly which are those that will have to be paid back in the near future, either by plan or by foreclosure?
2. What are the assets of the company, and what are the approximate values and liquidity of those assets? This assessment may change dramatically as the rescue progresses.
3. What is the net value of the company? This is a key measure for establishing how long a rescue attempt has to work and, one hopes, a measure that will change as the rescue progresses.

CASH FLOW BUDGET AND CONTROL SYSTEM

In its simplest form this will look like the proforma shown in Table 7.4.

Table 7.3. Balance sheet

Short-term funds		*Current assets*	
Bank overdraft		Cash	
Creditors and accrued charges		Debtors (1)	
Hire purchase outstanding		Inventory (1)	
Taxation payable		S. T. investments (1)	
Loans for up to one year			
Pension if due for investment			
	A		E
Long-term funds			
Bank loans			
Other loans for over one year			
Loan stock			
Deferred taxation			
Pension fund if not to be invested			
	B		
Permanent capital			
Preference capital			
	C		
Ordinary share capital		*Fixed assets*	
Ordinary shares		Goodwill (2)	
Profit & loss account		Land and buildings (3)	
Share premium account		Plant and machinery (3)	
Capital reserve		Vehicles (3)	
Depreciation reserve		L. T. investments	
Other reserves & provisions set up to meet future liabilities (e.g. bad debts reserve)		Sub-let property (3)	
	D		F

Total capital	A+B+C+D
Long-term capital	B+C+D
Permanent capital	C+D
Equity funds	D
Current assets	E
Fixed assets	F
Total assets	E+F

(1) Balance sheet value greater than real value (also probably true for all fixed assets)
(2) Probably should be zero
(3) Ideally should be analysed by location and/or profit centre

Table 7.4. Cash flow budget proforma

Month	Jan.	Feb.	...	Nov.	Dec.	Total
Cash in						
Cash sales						
Debtors						
VAT						
Realisation of assets						
Loans receivable						
Other receipts						
Asset sales						
Other						
Cash inflow						
Cash out						
Utilities						
Suppliers						
VAT						
Wages & salaries by dept						
PAYE and Employers NIC						
Capital expenditure						
Taxation						
Rental and leases						
Loan interest						
Loan repayments						
Other payments						
Cash outflow						
Net cash flow						
Bank balance						

As the sophistication and in-company experience of the controller/financial director increases, each of the major variables will be analysed by physical/management cause. The most important aspects of this particular budget are as follows:

1. It identifies the principal sources and uses of cash.
2. It is used to set properly rigorous targets.
3. Performance is measured against it, regularly and promptly.
4. Action is taken to correct any shortfall, and the outcomes of that action are in turn monitored.

The example given is an aggregate budget. It should be made up from subordinate budgets that fit with accountability for each of the component parts, and (unlike the profits budget) should be updated and reviewed on a monthly basis, since it gives advance warning of potentially terminal financing problems.

COST ANALYSIS

Initially cost analysis can concentrate on major items only, dealing with detail areas later. As well as considering the conventional cost classifications, give thought to assessing by the following categories, when relevant, if they are not already known.

Variable vs *fixed cost*

Determining variable costs as opposed to fixed costs is important for analysing the effect of volume changes on the overall costs of the business, and therefore the effect on profitability.

Traceable vs *common (allocated) cost*

This category is very important to understand how accurate is the classification of variable costs and fixed costs. Traceable costs can be identified with individual products; common costs cannot, and they are relatively arbitrarily allocated to products.

Incremental vs *marginal (and variable) costs*

Marginal (and variable) costs tend to be calculated on the basis of the unit effect of small volume changes. Major changes, or complete product cancellations, can alter dramatically the fixed costs, setup costs, and so forth, so that incremental cost must be assessed.

Escapable vs *inescapable costs*

When ceasing an activity it is important to consider whether all the costs will be saved. For example, interest costs on unrepaid loans after closure of a factory with little terminal value are broadly inescapable.

Cash vs *book cost*

The biggest distinction between book cost and cash is with depreciation, which can overstate the cash effect of losses.

Committed vs *discretionary costs*

Committed costs are those we have no choice but to incur to stay in business at our current capacity; discretionary (or managed) costs, like advertising or research, are not essential. In turnarounds, a bigger proportion of costs is discretionary than most are willing to believe, and it can be reduced by more than most are willing to accept.

Standby vs *enabling cost*

Standby and enabling costs are subdivisions of committed cost. Standby costs are incurred irrespective of whether the capacity is used (depreciation, insurance); enabling costs are incurred only when capacity is used.

The preceding are just a few useful cost categorisations that lead to important questions being posed. Clearly when radical changes are being considered, as in any rescue, considerable thought needs to go in to how to present, and think about, accounting data to provide proper decision support.

With cheap computer technology available, it is well worthwhile modelling both physical and financial processes to help formulate tactics and strategy to cut costs and maximise profits. This exercise can give enormously valuable insights, as I described about a particular operation in the *Sloan Management Review*:

All these applications occurred within a period of less than eight months.

A commodity that could not be perfectly hedged accounted for a major portion of the cost of our products. This commodity had a significant impact on the cost of production, could materially affect the contribution on sales, and, in conjunction with currency and other commodity movements, could cause a major shift in the location of the most profitable marketplace. The price of this commodity had to be followed closely. Although this was possible, but time-consuming, on a manual basis, the personal computer made it easy to evaluate the current position more rapidly and to explore the various probabilities in detail. Because rapid moves between markets were difficult without causing disruptive effects on customers and running the risk of competitor retaliation, this was partly calculated and partly an intuitive decision. Our exploratory analysis involved calculating the quantitative aspects of the probable scenarios and making judgements about the rest. Typically, the process, including our discussion, took ten minutes.

Complex catalysts accounted for an important portion of our costs and represented a significant competitive advantage or penalty when used well or poorly. To make the best use of these catalysts tradeoffs had to be made between capacity, cost, and output flexibility. The first two involved a very complex calculation, and the last called for a very difficult judgement as the market was very competitive and highly seasonal. The inability to adjust the output up or down at short notice could start minor or major price wars in the effort to maintain volume. Our decision making involved running many alternatives on the computer and selecting the option that offered the best risk/return using cost curves from the computer and our intuitive judgement of the market consequences of each possible action.

We were able to recover a significant proportion of our raw material costs by selling by-products on a commodity basis. Based on the price per pound, it seemed that we were maximising our return.

However, by using a linear programming model, we determined that a dramatic improvement in revenues could be achieved by investing a small amount of money to change the product mix. This evaluation required many calculations since the change in production was significant, and each run involved a test of feasibility for either the new markets or the proposed new production method. In addition, the implications for our competitors also had to be assessed. It was a highly interactive, iterative process.

The marginal costs of production did not follow a linear pattern or anything that approximated a linear function. They were a function of both aggregate volume and the effects of interaction between product lines; many of the cost components had complex volume relationships in their own right. The results of the analysis, however, had major strategic implications for the company.

All of the above applications share some common features. All allowed profit improvements of at least half a million dollars per year; all were essentially interactive, exploratory processes involving the exercise of judgement; and none could have been done without accessible computing power. It is relatively easy to accurately quantify the benefits of using personal computers in these applications. This list of examples is, of course, by no means exhaustive. Other applications would illustrate such additional benefits as:

The advantages gained in the budgeting process through the rapid access and manipulation of large amounts of data;
The increase in the usefulness of variance analysis due to high speed access to explanatory data;
The enormous increase in comprehension made possible by a major production and marketing data base;
The speed and ease of use provided by graphical presentation of data.[32]

Ten years ago some of the sophisticated techniques described here, such as linear programming, would have been hopelessly ponderous and time consuming. Today they are relatively easy to use, employing package software. The main limitation is the availability of the raw data.

PRODUCT COSTINGS

Table 7.5 shows a typical ex-factory-product cost recovery sheet. It can be as shown, or on a per-unit basis, and/or against budget. It is the simplest of documents and yet is very useful for both cost control and pricing. This one is for a manufacturing concern; a similarly simple form could easily be designed for a retail operation (based on sales and margin per square foot of space), a transport operation (per vehicle) and so on. However, where production labour is a key cost, a cost comparison statement like Table 7.6 could be used. None of these is complex; neither do they take long to set up. For these, as for the more complex techniques described earlier, the critical consideration is simply collecting accurate raw data.

Table 7.5. Statement of cost recovery

		Variable cost				
Product	Sales value	Materials	Labour	Overheads	Total	Margin
Total						
					Fixed costs for period	
					Profit for period	

Source: R. Powell in *Handbook of Financial Management*, No. 13 (Kluwer Publishing Ltd).

Similar comments apply to other operational control systems. Often a host of information resides in sales reports, complaint reports, pricing summaries, quality control analyses, process control summaries, energy summaries and the like. The information is often there in abundance but simply needs to be turned into English and reduced to a summary form. At this stage one good-quality cost accountant can be worth his weight in gold.

Table 7.6. Cost comparison statement

	Hours worked			Wage rate factor	Cost				Total variance	Analysis of variance		
	Budget	Allowed	Actual		Budget	Revised	Allowed	Actual		Wage rate	Volume	Efficiency
Production labour												
TOTAL												
Variable overheads controlled by department												
Lost time												
Overtime premium												
National insurance												
Holiday pay												
Loose tools and consumable stores												
Scrap and rectification												
Maintenance												
X												
X												
Total variable overheads												
Fixed overheads												
Supervision												
Clerical salaries												
Indirect labour												
Depreciation												
Total fixed overheads												
Total costs												

Notes: 1. Details of Production labour could be broken down into production groups, cost centres, types of labour, etc.
2. 'Allowed' hours worked would be the standard hours for the actual production.
3. 'Wage rate factor' represents the weighted average rate per man hour for the group in question divided by the budgeted average rate, and multiplied by 100.
4. 'Revised' wages cost represents the allowed hours priced at the budgeted wage rate.
5. 'Allowed' wages cost represents the allowed hours priced at the revised wage rate factor.
6. Total variance is the difference between the budgeted and actual cost.
7. 'Wage' rate variance is the difference between the 'Revised' and 'Allowed' cost.
8. 'Volume' variance is the difference between the budgeted wages and the 'Allowed' wages.
9. 'Efficiency' variance is the difference between the total variance and the total of the other two variances.
10. 'Allowed' variable overheads are calculated by multiplying the budgeted figure by the 'Allowed' hours divided by the budgeted hours.

Source: R. Powell in *Handbook of Financial Management*, No. 13 (Kluwer Publishing Ltd).

Major strategies

At each stage of the recovery programme one or more of the following strategies will be undertaken:

1. Asset reduction.
2. Cost reduction.
3. Improved marketing (in its widest sense, including product innovation).
4. Investment.

Where to put the emphasis is a matter of considerable judgement.

Steady-state improvements are generally achieved in operating terms by cost reduction strategies, revenue-generating strategies, or strategies involving redirection of the company's efforts. Some highly skilled turnaround experts recommend general rules to guide whether to favour cost reduction or revenue-generation strategies or some combination of the two. Charles Hofer, for example, suggests that companies that are close to their breakeven point in sales are good candidates for cost-cutting strategies, while companies that are only between 30% and 60% of their breakeven point should aim for a revenue-generating and asset reduction strategy. Figure 7.2 highlights exactly what he means by this.

It is preferable to look at all the strategies under any circumstances and to assess each proposal on its merits. It may be that a company that is close to its breakeven in revenue is still capable of significant revenue increases.

ASSET REDUCTION PROGRAMMES

Which assets?

The decision on which assets to dispose of is divided neatly into the obvious and the not at all obvious. Amongst the obvious fall the dross – fixed and current assets that are obsolete or for some reason useless to the company; the surplus – such as under-utilised factories, office blocks, depots, not to mention idle inventory; and the cash haemorrhagers. The last category consists of those areas that cause significant cash outflow to the company. In the end, these will be disposed of at any price possible, since their disposal in fact improves the company's position; but obviously in the first instance the highest price should be sought.

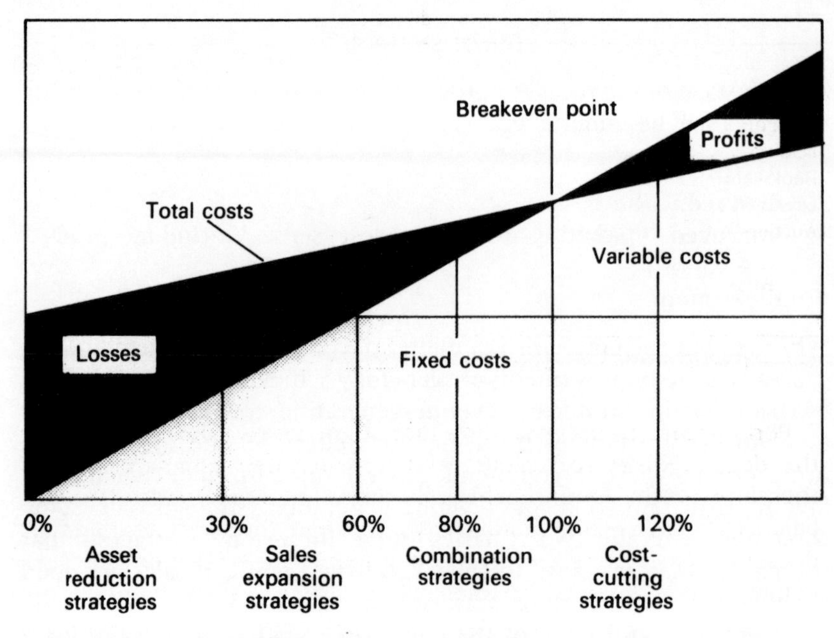

Source: Charles Hofer, *Advanced Management Report*, vol. 2, no. 1 (1980).

Fig. 7.2. Breakeven point as a guide to strategies.

The not so obvious group, which is more difficult, may be categorised as either 'can be done cheaper' or inadequate return on disposal value. 'Can be done cheaper' refers simply to those parts of the business that are operating from excessively expensive property or with excessively expensive assets. Cost effectiveness is the key criterion here. The most common example of this is the use of prestige office space, and it is of course the easiest solved. Other examples include retail outlets in overly expensive high street locations whose performance does not justify their capital commitment, and old and often obsolete factories based in the centre of towns and cities. It is quite often possible to recapitalise an obsolete plant by selling the land on which it stands and opening a new factory outside town, often in a development area. If it is not possible to relocate the plant, if it sits on a valuable asset, the property may still be worth selling. In this circumstance the decision is the straightforward outcome of calculating the return on disposal value that is earned by the plant, both in profit and cash terms. It should be noted from the US experience that usually assets are divested for very close to book value (see Table 7.7).

Table 7.7 Value of divested assets received

Value	% received
Full going concern value	7
Less than going concern, more than book value	10
Book value	53
Less than book value, more than auction value	5
Auction or liquidation value	25
Total	100

Source: Donald B. Bibeault, *Corporate turnaround* (McGraw Hill, 1982), p.246.

Perhaps one in six can achieve more than book value, typically when the deal involves real estate, and one in three achieves less. It is therefore worth examining the real value of the assets to ensure that the balance sheet does not dramatically understate (or overstate) them. If it does, then calculating the return on disposal value – meaning the profit before interest and tax divided by the total disposal values net of redundancy costs – both now and after some management action has been taken to improve the returns should clearly indicate whether disposal is necessary.

There is a natural scale of time to the various types of disposal. Separable assets such as subsidiary companies, underperforming depots, branches, and surplus fixed and current assets can all be sold in the relatively short term. Assets such as land on which there are operating factories are clearly much longer term issues. Nevertheless, this matter should be kept in review. Although asset reduction is an innate part of the early stages of a company rescue, maintaining the high level of utilisation of assets and the proper deployment of assets is a significant part of remaining competitive.

At the later stages, as financial pressures ease, some qualitative factors come into play. Perhaps the most important of these is a decision as to what constitutes core business and what constitutes peripheral business in the running of the company. This complex strategic judgement involves a number of factors, including how much management effort goes into running the relevant operations of the company, how close the skill needs of the operation are to the basic skills of the company, whether the operation supports other parts of the company in terms of marketing effort or technology, and whether the operation absorbs or generates cash on a significant scale. Thus, a cash generator that is a critical part of the crisis-recovery stage but that has no overlap with other parts of the company may well be kept for the first two years and then sold in a judicious and profit-maximising manner once the rest of the company is on a stable base.

The disposal process

Today there are specialist companies that do a very good job of selling off parts of companies, whether they be real estate or fully fledged subsidiaries. As a general rule such professionals raise a larger sum of money than would normally be obtained by a manager doing this as a one-off exercise. Marketing skills count for a great deal in this area, but most managers do not have the experience to develop such skills. Nevertheless, it is worthwhile reviewing briefly the questions that have to be asked. The first, most simple questions are these:

1. *Exactly* what is being sold?
2. To whom is this most valuable?
3. What is the value to the buyer?
4. What is the value to the seller?

Answering these questions is straightforward if what is being sold is a piece of land or a building and an estate agent will do most of the work. If it is something more complex, such as a business, an investment bank can help enormously in the process. A miminum disposal value should be determined, but it should not be disclosed to the advisers at this stage. It is often valuable to write a prospectus of the disposal company before estimating its worth to the proposed customer.

Essentially one is aiming for the best of current asset value *or* future profit stream *or* future cash flow stream for the purchaser. Tax benefits should not be overlooked; neither should all the advantages of the merger accounting rules. We are interested only in the cash, but if we do not take into account all the benefits to the customer we may well end up either underpricing what is being sold or missing a potential customer (which amounts to the same thing).

The advantage of multiple buyers should not be underestimated either. Very few negotiators are as good as the auction process for getting the last ounce of value out of a would-be purchaser. In addition, the process is by no means mutually exclusive. These days it is common practice to have an auction to determine the two top bidders and then to negotiate up from their supposedly final bid.

Management issues

As a rule it is preferable to bring on board very early the top manager in the unit being sold. This inspires confidence, for although the news may not be pleasing for him to hear, he cannot avoid recognising that to keep him informed at this point is an exercise in trust. One mechanical point of security should not be overlooked, however. The manager should be told the news face to face, not in writing, nor over the telephone.

Communication should also preferably be off site so that the manager is not inclined to tell anyone in the 15 minutes after he has heard what is possibly shocking news. He should be told where the conversation is unlikely to be overheard (which is *not* true of offices). For as long as the information is confidential, he should be discouraged from discussing the matter over the telephone from his office or writing about it.

There is one other advantage in informing the management early, and that is to do so may precipitate a management buy-out (MBO). In a surprising number of cases this will generate the highest sale price for an asset. Indeed, the cynical might comment that it is remarkable how often management can do nothing with assets until they own them, or a portion of them, themselves. For this reason, where a management buy-out is proposed, consider at least a second pass of the viability of the asset concerned to see whether the value can be extracted for the current investors, rather than for the management and the management buy-out financiers. Nevertheless, an MBO still may be worthwhile, though it is difficult to generate the sort of motivation in managers that a second mortgage inspires. In fact, it may well be worth while precipitating such a thought oneself, perhaps after a brief discussion with one of the financial institutions that supports such an exercise. In Britain, typically Citibank, Charterhouse, 3i and Globe Investment Trust (Candover) are some of the leaders in the field.

Sale and leaseback

It is unlikely, but possible, that the company has property that could reasonably be sold and leased back and that is not subject to the first call of the bank or other lending institutions. This is a hazardous exercise at best because, although it generates immediate cash, it reduces that asset base of the company and increases its fixed cost level. This latter effect is not only bad for cashflow in the medium term; it also has a very bad effect on the company's competitive behaviour. This is a mechanism of last resort.

Working capital reduction

In practice there are two ways of achieving reduction of working capital: by reducing inventories and by reducing debtors.

Reducing inventories

1. *Stopping current deliveries.* Inventories can be reduced by stopping purchasing (the conventional method), cancelling orders in progress, and/or refusing delivery of goods, and returning goods that have recently been delivered. As we are the customer in this context, there is very little that cannot be done; although given that our credit rating is poor, we will have to be careful with suppliers upon whom we critically depend.
2. *Increase order frequency/reduce order size.* Often ordering frequency is a function of what is convenient to the manager concerned rather than a sophisticated calculation of economic order quantity. Irrespective of this, as a cash-generating mechanism, more frequent orders are a worthwhile way of reducing average inventory. Indeed, order size may be reduced *below* economic order quantity because of the need to buy *time.*
3. *Negotiate with the supplier to hold stocks on our behalf.* This is a particularly valuable method if we are a large customer for the supplier and he is anxious to keep our trade. It is in effect a low-risk way for the supplier to extend extra credit to us. This method might well be negotiated in conjunction with paying off a portion of our standing account.
4. *Sell off obsolete or very low turnover stock.* One of the grim facts of most companies is that a proper audit of the inventory shows up a need to write-off a large proportion of stock that has been held for too long. Obsolete stock costs money to keep; it takes space, management, and capital; and it only gets less valuable. It should be sold off *immediately.*
5. *Review stock control systems.* This approach is particularly effective for work in progress. Also to be analysed is how the production scheduling systems depend on stock control systems and affect them. One of the remarkable characteristics of Japanese plants is that they operate with considerably lower stocks of work in progress than a typical Western plant. Not only is this more efficient in the use of capital, it also imposes a rigorous and effective discipline on the production staff. It is one of the reasons that zero defect quality control systems and just-in-time purchasing procedures work very well in Japan.

6. *Introduce special promotions and discount schemes to clear old finished goods inventory*. Quite often the history of bad results makes management nervous of taking any further write-offs. In one factory in which I worked, the management authorised the reprocessing of a 100-tonne batch of glucose seven times to try to get it up to quality. Each time they failed, just missing the quality control standards; the batch then deteriorated in store for a month until it had to be reprocessed again. It must have been the most expensive glucose in the world, but it got sold as molasses at a quarter of the final price within a month of my arrival. Despite the unpleasant write-off, the clearance was by far the most economic thing to do and had the useful psychological side effect of allowing the production teams to get on with making a product first time around.

Reducing debtors

The most powerful cash generation programme in existence is the implementation of a proper debtor age analysis, and the use of a telephone to act upon it. This does not have to be an unpleasant process, and indeed the ideal person to implement the collection is someone with a pleasant telephone manner. Very often inefficiency in the company's collection department is matched only by inefficiency in the customer's processing department. The only difference is that their inefficiency works in their favour, not ours. Certainly 80% of customers will pay if reminded promptly and if it is pointed out to them they are very much overdue on the terms of their contract. The tougher nuts can be filtered out in this way and dealt with by a more senior and tougher credit controller, or in the end by the finance director or financial vice-president. Two methods can be used to encourage debtors to pay up, as follows:

1. *Factoring*. This is a route to be taken only if both the accounts and sales departments of the company are in such a terrible state that they cannot cope with it themselves. Factoring is expensive, and it introduces an unknown into the relationship with the customer, with potentially unpleasant and certainly unpredictable results. It should be done only as a last resort.
2. *Changing payment terms*. The simple gambit of giving a discount against payment on time can be introduced at price increase time. So long as the price increase is calculated to cover the discount, nobody loses, but the customer is encouraged to pay on time. This is a delicate area and has to be handled carefully. However, with a

sales force of any competence, one can point out to the good customers who pay on time that they will lose nothing; it is those who are the poor customers not paying on time who will resist this, but they are likely to have problems anyway. Nevertheless, this step must be carried out with care.

Asset reduction strategies in the early stages of the recovery simply create room to manoeuvre and fulfil a bailing-out function, albeit a vital one. In the later stages, although important as a method of improving efficiency and as an internal source of generating capital, they are not the most fundamental long-term components of the turnaround. Only if the rescue is of a company that has over diversified, over borrowed, or got into trouble by building a major capital project that has overrun its budget, is an asset reduction or redeployment strategy appropriate by itself.

COST REDUCTION STRATEGIES

The first action to be undertaken as a part of the cost reduction strategy is a simply Pareto analysis of the company's costs. In other words, rank the costs in order of size. Pareto's Law, which is also known as the 80–20 rule, says that for most aspects of business life 80% of the importance (of, for example, sales, costs, cash) is accounted for by 20% of the categories (for example, customers, locations, managers, cost categories). A ranking of the cost categories by size will, for most companies, show that ten categories cover the vast majority of a company's costs. The next stage in the analysis is to look through the costs and determine what impact can be made upon them. This may change the ranking dramatically.

For example, a company might buy a commodity at a price that is fixed in one of the commodity markets (such as sugar, maize, wheat, silver or copper). The extent to which one can control these costs is limited and requires sophisticated knowledge of the markets concerned, with large information systems that guide when to time one's purchases. They are also affected by complex trade-offs between lowest cost purchasing and 'hedged' or low-risk purchasing. Other areas, such as company car policy or advertising, may make up a much smaller proportion of the company's expenses, but they are virtually entirely controllable.

The new chief executive should determine which he considers to be his top ten costs and maintain a control file that lives in his desk or briefcase. The file might include a weekly purchase summary and monthly accounts. He should also know precisely who is accountable for each category of expenditure. Just the existence of such a file has a persuasive and constructive effect on the accountable managers.

The first emergency stage generally involves such things as a freeze on hiring, with the chief executive's personal approval required for any increases or replacements of personnel. It may well involve a freeze on other discretionary expenditure, particularly that of the most visible sort. For example, all company car replacements may be deferred to give an immediate cash advantage. Certainly any visibly extravagant schemes such as office redecorations will immediately be halted. Advertising expenditures might be stopped, at least until their effectiveness is reviewed. This stage has two purposes: one is to achieve real savings; the other is to create the climate in which savings can be made.

While all this is happening a number of other preparatory stages are going on. Sound costing and cost control systems will be implemented. The checklist in Table 7.2 gives some idea of the guidelines that might be used for such systems. Similarly, purchasing would be under severe review and, again'a checklist (see Table 7.8 on page 114) gives some indications of the sort of approach that would be necessary.

Also during the early part of the crisis stage of rescue the historical review of costs and a cost reduction feasibility study should be continued. Every cost category should be linked to its associated output, and its changes over the previous few years should be assessed, both on an absolute and on a unit-cost basis. Competitors' costs may not be available, in which case one will need to compare the costs movements with competitor prices. Although this has all the dangers of using averages, it at least gives a reference point that is better than that of general inflation. For general inflation does not reflect the learning and efficiency improvements that ought to happen in most normal companies over time. Neither does it reflect the necessary responses.

These preliminary studies should focus particularly upon overheads and manpower. Overheads generally are promising areas for cost reduction, partly because they tend to proliferate in sloppily run organisations, partly because computerisation ought to enable them to be reduced, though in practise often does not, and also partly because any mistakes made in cost reduction in this sector will have the least effect on the company's market or production position.

Manpower should be looked at for two reasons. Firstly, in most businesses it is a very significant cost category in its own right. Apart from the direct cost, it typically carries a large number of ancillary costs with it, some of which typically are measured (such as National Insurance) and some of which are not (such as the cost of personnel department, payroll, canteens, and parking spaces and all the other benefits that go with employment). Secondly, quite reasonably, people balk at the unpleasant decision of cutting back on workers and having redundancy programmes. Although this squeamishness is perfectly understandable, it is a luxury that a company facing failure cannot afford. That people do balk at such decisions means there is probably excess manpower in the company.

Overhead reduction

Most overhead reductions require three things:

1. A reasonably well defined sense of direction that the company is about to take.
2. Involvement of knowledgeable middle management.
3. A forced timetable, preferably associated with some physical change.

The first requirement is needed simply to dictate the emphasis of the overhead cuts. In most rescue attempts cuts are made in all departments; but if it is intended to revamp the marketing effort, radically reducing the size of the marketing department immediately may not be sensible. Similarly, should quality control or production scheduling seem to be key areas for effort, they may be protected or even increased.

The involvement of knowledgeable management is simply to ensure that the most efficient job is done. Quite stunning reductions are possible in some circumstances, often exceeding 50% of previous costs. Often this is achieved by cutting out the extraneous activity that was never previously challenged (such as the rarely read report), often by streamlining and reduction of double handling of documentation, sometimes by delegation of staff functions to operational supervisors, sometimes by computerisation, and sometimes by just pure simplification. Alternatively, it may be possible to 'buy in' the service, or buy that part for which there is variable demand; this approach can be appropriate for everything from the company legal department to the company print shop, from the company canteen to the office cleaner. This list is just illustrative, but it does demonstrate the importance of detailed knowledge of the company's systems and procedures in devising such improvements.

The final requirement of a forced timetable is necessary to get the best results in the optimum time. This can occasionally be quite artificial. It can also be quite arbitrary. I once rented out half of a floor space of the head office of a transport company to somebody else, with the tenancy to take effect four months hence. It focused and precipitated a long overdue overhead reduction, which led initially to irritation and discomfort; but after three months of operating in a reduced area with fewer people, morale was higher than it had ever been.

With all reductions in personnel the ideal outcome is to be able to keep the very best staff and lose the weakest. This is doubly true in staff departments for maximising quality of work and work rate, which often solely depend upon the individual, and which can have a vital highly geared effect upon the company's success or failure. It is particularly important to protect the key information system and control systems upon which the overall recovery will depend.

Clearly, this section (and the next) describes unpleasant processes. Nobody in his right mind enjoys taking away people's jobs. Doing so is justifiable only because it protects the remaining jobs and because it ensures that the company can go on making a valuable contribution to society.

It should also be understood, however, that frequently a marked improvement in morale takes place when such rationalisations are carried out. In the transport company cited earlier, for example, overhead reductions had clearly been necessary for at least a year prior to rescue and the whole atmosphere had been soured by the perpetual expectation of the job cuts about to come. This atmosphere was worsened by the fact that many people were underemployed and therefore had a great deal of time to worry and gossip about the poor management that was causing all their problems. The result of the programme was shock when it was announced, irritation when it was first implemented and a very sharp rise in morale within a few months of that implementation. This rise in morale occurred partly because people were working harder, which is actually normally an enjoyable process, partly because the insecurity in their future for *them* had been removed, and partly because the company had a clear sense of direction and leadership. This is a common syndrome in company recoveries.

The final point to note in people-related exercises is that even more than for other cost reduction exercises it is vitally necessary once the cost reduction has been achieved to maintain and improve on the position by rigorous discipline. This means that as time passes a continuous downward pressue on the number of people employed should be maintained. As people leave, the job should be met by redeployment of current personnel as far as possible, rather than by replacement from outside. This not only keeps up constant pressure for improved efficiency and productivity, it also dramatically reduces the likelihood of a subsequent radical reduction being made. In turn this creates a better climate of security of employment, which improves morale and dramatically improves the level of co-operation in further productivity improvement programmes. Once established, this can be a very valuable virtuous cycle.

Labour reduction exercises

As discussed, often it is necessary to undertake a programme of manpower reduction and productivity improvement in recovery companies. This of course is the norm in many companies today. The only difference is that in a recovery company the demands are much higher and generally involve a step change rather than a gradual change.

The advantage that management has in a recovery company (if it can be seen as an advantage) is that it is operating in visibly harsh circumstances. If these circumstances are perceived by the workforce as a real threat to jobs, then the bargaining position of the management is much more powerful than is usual. It is possible to have discussions and negotiations in a language and environment of harsh realities far removed from the normal rhetoric of such exercises.

It may be, however, that a previous management has given many warnings in the past but never actually acted on any of them. If so, the workforce and trade unions will quite reasonably view with great scepticism the claims of hardship put up by the company. This is particularly so because the middle management, who will be the main communicators of these messages, will probably be the same people that the workforce has disbelieved before. If that is the case, it is easy to slip back into the traditional contest of mindless machismo that does neither side any good. Under these circumstances the new chief executive has two weapons at his disposal, action and information.

Likely when he arrives in the company, the chief executive will have clear in his mind the need to do one or two difficult things. Typically these may well involve the firing of some of the senior management, either because of demonstrable incompetence in the past or because their responsibilities are going to be reduced to nothing by the rationalisation programme. In general these will be only the most obvious decisions, since they will have been visible to the chief executive from outside the organisation. If that is the case, they will also have been obvious to virtually everybody inside the organisation for a very long time. Since these actions would have to be taken at some time anyway, they can be used to demonstrate both the seriousness of the situation and the determination of the management. If, say, trade union officials see the new chief executive arrive, and instead of blustering about the problems he faces and the sacrifices their members will have to make he quickly gets rid of one or two of the most incompetent members of the management team and closes down or sells off the most inefficient parts of the company, they are likely to take him much more seriously. This apparently callous action is likely to change the climate and so improve the probability of intelligent and productive deals and reduce the risk of outright strikes. It will accordingly have a beneficial effect on the job security of those people whose employment is rescuable.

It is important to ensure that this action is, and is seen as, toughness rather than unreasonableness. The key here is information. Proper explanation to the staff and workforce through a briefing group should be supported by proper information given to the trade union to explain the circumstances of the company and the reasons for the harsh actions.

If the chief executive envisages a major redundancy programme, he should not underestimate how much planning will be required to carry it through. The planning will be difficult for a variety of reasons. Firstly, it will have to be carried out in great secrecy, with a limited number of managers involved. Secondly, it will be venturing into areas where few of the managers have any experience. Thirdly, it will have to be robust in the face of negotiating demands from the trade union and the workforce. That planning will have to cover a number of areas, as follows:

The size of workforce reductions

In assessing the size of reductions, the planner will have to take into account what is physically possible, what is necessary for the survival of the company, what the competition manages, and what is judged to be acceptable without a strike.

Timing

In general speed is preferable, both for the purposes of morale and useful cost reduction. Arguments will be marshalled about the practicality of doing things too quickly; unless there is demonstrable physical reason (such as the necessary arrival of a new piece of capital equipment), these arguments for delay and slowness should be resisted.

Information
It is important to manage the briefing of other management, workforce, and trade unions to a detailed timetable, often with simultaneous briefing of several plants. The press and other media should not be forgotten in this exercise, since public acceptability may well dictate long-term feelings about the actions and indeed influence trade union responses.

Compensation
Compensation is a difficult subject to advise on *in vacuo*. There will of course be legal minima, but in addition to this the management will have to decide whether or not to give more than is required either by the legal or contract terms. On the one hand large redundancy payments make the process socially tolerable and easier to implement, but on the other the company is unlikely to be in a position to hand out a lot of cash to the departing workforce. It is a difficult balance to judge, although I tend towards generosity both for ethical and practical reasons.

Relocation
If at all possible, some attempt should be made to help find new work for as many of the redundant employees as possible. Sometimes other local companies will take on a limited number of a particularly vulnerable group; IBM, for example, once agreed to complete the training of the apprentices for a unit that I had to close in Greenock. Local companies are often remarkably altruistic if their help is sought.

Legal considerations
Employment and trade union law is clearly a significant and important component of the planning process here. It is, however, changing dramatically, and so different from country to country that commenting upon it is more appropriate for a magazine than a book. However, clearly the law has to be taken into account.

Training
It is of no use having a dramatic reduction in labour costs if the factory is not able to run in the immediate aftermath. Apart from its direct financial effects, such an outcome would have a crippling effect upon workforce morale and severely undermine the credibility of the management. And rightly so. The analysis of the old and new work patterns, the itemisation of the differences, and the provision of proper training will enable the workforce to cope with the changeover and is extremely important.

Physical issues
Apart from the proper calculation of matters such as holiday cover, weekend cover, and proper shift rotas, it is worth giving a good deal of thought to minor phsyical changes that will make the job easier. Woodruff Imberman's work on the causes of strikes showed clearly the importance of matters such as poor maintenance support on the night shift in destroying morale and increasing militancy.[33] Often worthwhile is polling the workforce to determine what problems they see as most irritating and problematic in terms of doing their job. Such a questionnaire will often prove very informative and can be a useful way of pinpointing areas where extra effort will yield large dividends. This is an area wherein over-resourcing is worthwhile, if it ever is.

Other major cost reductions

Purchasing
Table 7.8 gives a list of the sort of matters to be reviewed in improving purchasing and achieving cost reductions through that route.

Again, remember that the negotiating relationship with the suppliers is one in which they in many cases are at risk of losing a significant customer. Accordingly, it should be possible to obtain from them improvements in price, quality, design, delivery, stockholding levels, indeed virtually everything except credit. The principal levers to be used in this negotiation are the continued use of the supplier as a source and regular payment. Both are at risk in the period running up to the negotiation.

Efficiency improvement methods
Each of the methods detailed here is appropriate in certain circumstances.

1. *Value analysis and process and/or product design*. The objectives of value analysis are to:

    (a) determine the aim and use of the product for the customer;
    (b) examine how this aim is achieved;
    (c) examine alternative methods of achieving this aim, and determine their costs; and
    (d) devise new methods and/or designs to achieve the aim at minimum cost and maximum quality.

Table 7.8. Purchasing checklist

Costs

1. Are prices competitive (given quality levels)?
2. Does a policy exist for inviting bids (or estimates or tenders)?
3. Are quotations obtained from a sufficient number of sources?
4. Is there sufficient information on cost elements to know the reasonableness of prices charged?
5. Is the supplier carrying out unnecessary operations on the components he is supplying? (Are there operations that he could perform more economically than the buyer?) Is there scope for integration of activities?
6. What alternative materials have been considered?
7. Are the items being supplied patented? If not, can they be reproduced more cheaply by another source of supply?
8. Are make-or-buy studies undertaken? Are some components currently being made-in that could be bought-out at less cost?
9. Are economic factors other than price considered in selecting suppliers?
10. Are materials ordered in amounts and sizes that permit their utilisation with minimum wastage?
11. Is due consideration given to balancing ordering costs against stockholding costs? What are the cost implications of overdue deliveries?
12. What effect does storage have on materials? (Could the supplier hold stocks on behalf of the buying company?)
13. What controls do suppliers have over their activities? (For example, is standard costing employed? What are the quality control arrangements?)
14. Can we help the supplier improve his costs?
15. What credit terms are offered? (How do these compare with other suppliers' credit terms? How do they compare with the supplier's cash flow needs?)
16. Is the purchasing department given a sound forecast of materials and other requirements in good time to enable them to be bought on favourable terms?

Stocks

1. How are sales demanded? (daily, weekly)
2. In what quantities? (small lots, full loads)
3. Is the demand seasonal?
4. Are sales campaigns anticipated?
5. Has a desired service level been established?
6. Do we have too many stock points?
7. Do we control raw material, work in progress and finished stock?
8. Are these co-ordinated in any way?
9. Do we work with wholesalers, retailers, to balance their stocks?
10. Have we a forecasting system?
11. Is its success or failure monitored?
12. Do we monitor deterioration or obsolescence?
13. Is purchasing involved in phasing supplies of bought-in components?
14. Are subcontracted items actively controlled when only intermediate operations are necessary?
15. Do we monitor changing lead times with buyers?
16. Do predetermined order levels take this into account?

Table 7.8. (continued)

17. Has the order cost been identified?
18. Is production capacity identified?
19. Do we know all batch quantities to support a given level of production?
20. Is it possible to introduce 'consignment stocks', i.e. those financed by the supplier and paid for on a drawdown basis?

Quality and Security

1. Can the supplier meet quality standards?
2. Are suppliers' financial position and credit standing vetted?

Control

1. Are all purchase requisitions or purchase orders properly authorised?
2. Are safeguards in existence to prevent the purchasing of excessive quantities?
3. Do buyers have the authority to speculate in commodity markets?

Source: Derived from R. M. S. Wilson, *Cost control handbook.*

In essence, value analysis forces the product designer and/or process designer to consider the practical problems of producing exactly what the customer wants. In the context of a rescue we are looking for low cost or no cost solutions, and certainly ones that do not involve extra major capital investments. In the longer term this technique leads directly to the design of focused manufacturing systems, devised so as to give the best possible product from a customer's perspective at the minimum cost to the producer.

Value analysis and value engineering is very much a process that lends itself to a team approach. Often a team of aggressive young managers – including technical personnel; line manager(s); accountancy, purchasing and sales personnel – can achieve together what separately seemed impossible.

The example in Table 7.9 demonstrates what the process can do for a single operation. Although the absolute costs involved in this are trivial, the proportionate reduction is enormous. Applied across a whole process, this technique can yield enormous benefits.

2. *Materials usage and control.* Inefficiently run factories frequently waste considerably more material than is necessary. There are a variety of ways of dealing with this, including:

   (a) improved production scheduling to reduce downtime;
   (b) improved maintenance procedures also to reduce downtime (and in process plants, leakage);
   (c) improved design, where appropriate of the product;

Table 7.9. Example of a value analysis report

The following example illustrates the approach which value engineers use to eliminate the unnecessary. It is shown in the form of a report which could have been written by the value engineer on completion of the project.

Report on plug cover and attachments
Recommendations
A new method of carrying out the necessary functions of this cover has been devised which eliminates the need for the present cover and attaching fittings. The resulting yearly saving is £705 which is 84% of the present total cost of £835 per year. The cost of changeover to the new method will be about £270 which is easily offset by the savings during the first six months.

Functions
Primary function: to protect people who may be nearby in the event of the plug being blown out.
Secondary function: to protect the plug after assembly and during transport and use. To exclude entry of water or dirt once the plughole is open.

Present method
A domed, approximately hemispherical, spun metal cover is attached over the plug by means of six fittings and twelve bolts.

Proposal
The cover and fittings should be dispensed with and replaced by three lugs which are bolted to the container and shaped so as to trap the plug if it is blown out. This fulfils the primary function of the cover. The limited protection to the plug afforded by the lugs is considered to be adequate and the exclusion of water or dirt from the open plughole is not necessary since the containers will always be cleaned internally before refilling.

Cost comparison

The present method requires:	One cover	£2.45
	Six fittings	£1.35
	Twelve bolts	£1.20
	Total cost	£5.00 per assembly
The proposed method requires:	Three lugs	£0.48
	Three bolts	£0.30
	Total cost	£0.78 per assembly

The cost comparison includes the cost of assembly and fitting to the container. The saving will be £4.22 per assembly which on an annual usage of 167 assemblies results in a total annual saving of £705.

Changeover cost
Against this saving must be put the cost of design which is about £180, plus the cost of tool design and tooling costing another £90. The total changeover costs are thus £270.

Source: Chapter by Brian Piercy in *Financial management of production*, ed. Dennis Lock (Gower Press, 1975), p.150.

(d) the purchase of better quality, more appropriate or more appropriately sized materials;
(e) enhanced control of quality and quantity of incoming materials; or
(f) improved material handling – simple changes to process design are often very effective in this area. Where explicit waste is produced, what happens to this waste should be studied to see whether it could be recycled or sold for a higher price. Because this is unglamorous, it is frequently ignored.

3. *Zero defect style quality control.* People often consider higher quality to mean higher cost. Higher quality achieved through better organisation, better material control, better design and generally more effective management frequently costs considerably less than poor-quality operation. This is certainly true when recycling costs and marketing costs are taken into account properly.

   Many techniques have been tested in the last few years to determine quality, the most widely known being quality circles. Many of them act by encouraging the enthusiasm and commitment of the workforce to quality enhancement. This is a very sensible approach: it should not be seen as completely replacing the analytical and statistical methods developed previously, however. These methods all work best when they work together.
4. *De-bottlenecking/capacity planning/production control.* It is sometimes possible to achieve quite dramatic results by minor, or at least low-cost, changes of production organisation. For example, in one relatively high-tech plant that I ran it was possible to increase the output level by 30% as a result of using excessive design tolerance that was built into certain parts of the plant. By reorganising the plant to make maximum use of these tolerances, very cheap extra capacity was created. As well as providing extra revenue, this led to sharp reductions in unit costs, which in turn gave a significant competitive advantage. However, when assessing the possibilities in this area, it is a very good rule to beware averages. The statistical treatment of capacity design and management is quite complex and can be dealt with only by *detailed* study. The rewards are large, however.
5. *Budgetary control and zero base budgeting.* Tight budgetary control is the process by which costs are held in check and improved gradually over time. Normally this is not a technique used to achieve large cost reductions. A particular form of budget setting, however, called

'zero base budgeting', can be used to achieve quite dramatic reductions in costs. All that zero base budgeting is, is the commonsense procedure of challenging every cost category and in effect asking 'why do we do it at all, is there a better way, could it be done more cheaply, and why should this cost not be zero?' Hence zero base budgeting. One way or another, this process of challenge should be undertaken early in the recovery. The gains achieved with zero base budgeting are that it:

(a) ensures that every activity receives reappraisal and replanning, in concrete terms;
(b) focuses senior management attention on how best to allocate resources;
(c) communicates to the organisation that nothing is taken for granted; and
(d) encourages innovation by requiring managers to think of new and different approaches to their jobs.

Tight budgetary control is never more effective than when it is backed up by the stark alternative of corporate collapse.

Organising for cost reduction

Once we get beyond the obvious cutbacks, we require skill, determination and organisation to carry out major cost reduction. The skill lies in discovering where the current operation is inefficient and devising methods of rendering it more efficient. The determination is in finding the facts and challenging accepted wisdom to do this, in overcoming the organisation's resistance and persuading it to accept change, and finally in implementing that change. Organisation is firstly finding, or redeploying, people of sufficiently high quality to carry out the study and implement the changes; secondly, ensuring that the implementation is carried through; and thirdly, maintaining and improving on the benefits achieved over the longer term.

The technical skills may be within the organisation itself or the chief executive may have to import them by recruitment or use of consultants. But he himself will have to provide the determination and organisation.

The chapter on leadership refers to what the Americans call 'Tiger Teams'. Essentially highly motivated task forces, with the right blend of skills and plenty of energy, these teams are well suited to 'kickstarting' the cost reduction programme. They are also suitable for cracking intractable problems and fit well with the requirements of value-engineering exercises. Finally, they are first-class vehicles for testing the mettle of young managers to see if they are right for promotion. To succeed however, these teams must have the full-blooded and visible support and commitment of the chief executive. They will face passive resistance at least, and possibly aggressive opposition. They will need his backing.

In very short order, if not immediately, the cost improvement imperative must be forced into the organisation itself. Line managers will need to force the message home. Cost reduction – persistent cost reduction – is dependent on organisational determination.

IMPROVING MARKETING EFFECTIVENESS

This section interprets improving marketing effectiveness in its widest sense, to encompass anything that improves the level of revenue generated and the profitability of that revenue, and the defensibility of the market position. In approximate order of implementation the possible actions are as follows:

1. Reducing advertising and promotional activity.
2. Changing, generally increasing, prices.
3. Rationalising the product line.
4. Enhancing product, customer and/or geographical focus.
5. Improving selling effectiveness.
6. Improving customer value-for-money and quality perceptions.
7. Introducing feature, quality, service, and design differentiation.

Strategies of revenue enhancement are key to the success of a large number of turnarounds. Schendel and Patton's study showed that sales growth in successful turnaround was on average at least three times that in the other companies they studied. Revenue enhancement is also undoubtedly the most difficult part of a turnaround. It requires a strong combination of analysis, creativity and leadership.

Product analysis

The best place to start to determine the revenue enhancement strategy is with the compilation of as much product data as are available. Indeed it does no harm, if it is physically possible, to simply look at the product in comparison with two or three of its leading competitors. This should certainly be done with the top ten products if possible. Also enlightening is looking at some of the return product at the same time as reviewing a detailed analysis of returns and complaints. It is remarkable how often chief executives study reports in great detail without ever studying in similar detail what it is they sell.

This process of product review is often productively carried out in the presence of the marketing and manufacturing heads. One head of a car company in the United Kingdom used to do something similar. Every Monday morning he studied the worst car off the assembly line the previous week. The move was intended as a discipline for the production staff, but I suspect it also worked wonders in teaching everybody why their cars did not sell very well.

The next stop is the profit and loss accounts and factory costings for the products. Ideally it should be possible to obtain the marginal costs and full costs of production for each product or product line. If that is not available, the chief engineer, chief chemist, production manager, or whoever is best equipped should work out the following:

1. How much material, energy, and consumables *should* be used in manufacturing each product at (our) normal wastage rates?
2. How much labour cost goes into making each product?
3. How much machine time is used to manufacture each product, allowing for downtimes and changeovers?

With even such data, a competent cost accountant will be able to calculate roughly the variable cost of the products and he will be able to give a general indication of what the fixed-cost allocation ought to be. On this basis, order-of-magnitude contributions and net margins can be calculated.

This process in conjunction with the study of the complaints and volume trends should give the answers to the following questions:

1. Do we have distinctively different products from the competition?
2. Is the quality of our products distinctively better or worse?
3. Is the delivery service we give distinctively better or worse?
4. Are the answers to the above questions different for different product lines?
5. What are the volumes and volume trends of each product line?
6. What contribution to profit and overhead does each product line make?
7. Does manufacture of the line use up a disproportionate quantity of factory capacity, including downtimes for changeover?
8. Does the profit contribution of the product justify this quantity of capacity?

The answer to these questions should indicate the following:

1. Whether there has been an over-proliferation of products and product lines.
2. Which of those products should be pruned.
3. Which of those products should have their price increased.

In coming to a conclusion on pruning and price increases, we must look at the total cost of the product but at the same time be careful to ensure that we understand the method of allocation of overhead in arriving at our conclusions.

Competitor analysis

It is worth doing a summary checklist analysis of what the major competitors provide in the market place (see Table 7.10). It is generally quite easy to determine the competitors' product lines and their best-selling and weakest-selling items. This data can be backed up by a review of their pricing policy, their service levels and their quality levels. In this way identifying the strengths and weaknesses of a competitor and where the gaps are in his armour will tell us where to concentrate our marketing efforts and where to be most defensive.

The analysis used in this form is a useful discipline. For after analysing customer needs and competitor performance it often is easy to see *why* the market leaders *are* the market leaders. It is remarkable how clear cut the optimal strategy appears after such an analysis.

Customer analysis

Simple factual analysis is useful in understanding a customer's particulars. The points discussed in the sections that follow should be established.

Their importance to us

It is important to know if a class of customer accounts for a higher proportion of our profits, since this tells us the riskiness of any changes we undertake that affect them. It also establishes a guideline to how much effort we should put into maintaining their goodwill, providing them with a high-quality service and maintaining a high-frequency of follow-up calls.

Table 7.10. Assessment of the competition

Key competitive success factors		Your strengths		Your competitors' strengths							
Factors	Weights			Alpha		Beta		Gamma		Delta	
Technical quality	.30	10	3.00	8	2.40	6	1.80	3	.90	5	1.20
Price	.20	8	1.60	9	1.80	2	.40	10	2.00	5	1.00
Breadth of line	.15	7	1.05	9	1.35	4	.60	3	.45	3	.45
Distribution	.10	6	.60	9	.90	3	.30	5	.50	2	.20
Sales force	.10	7	.70	8	.80	4	.40	3	.30	3	.30
Customer service	.10	7	.70	4	.40	10	1.00	3	.30	2	.20
Reputation, image	.05	8	.40	10	.50	4	.20	2	.10	1	.05
Total strategic muscle	—	8.05		8.15		4.90		4.55		3.40	
Current market share	—	30%		40%		15%		10%		5%	

Source: Milton Shapiro, *Marketing News* (April 1980).

Our importance to them
There may be some customers for whom our product is extremely important. This can occur because our product is critical to their process or because it is a very large component of their cost. In the first instance this would imply a highly quality-driven marketing approach, possibly with high technical support; in the second it might imply price sensitivity on the part of the customer. Where our product is only a minor part of their purchases, however, it might imply that we have to advertise a great deal in order to get their attention for our product.

Alternatives
The alternatives available to the customer, in the form of either substitutes or competitive products, are the key to deciding the price that we charge. They can also have a major influence on technical support, service levels and quality.

Switching costs
The costs incurred in changing supplier can feature large in the marketing decisions made with respect to individual customers. Obviously the higher the switching costs, the higher the price one can afford to charge. However, one should not forget that switching costs work in both directions: a mistake or poor judgement on the pricing front will be difficult to reverse once we have lost the customer.

Perceived needs
What the customer sees as his needs can differ markedly from what the company thinks he wants. Within industrial products there is generally a specification, but there may also be an unknown agenda of items behind the specification that dictates the level of customer satisfaction. Delivery frequency, responsiveness, and qualitative factors such as how clean the delivery truck is and how polite the driver is can all have a significant impact. Often a detailed analysis of the complaints can give some insight into this area. This is the most difficult area of marketing and is responsible for some of the most brilliant successes, and the most abject failures. If I were able to give one skill, not just to the marketing manager but to the chief executive of a company, it would be the ability to understand precisely what his customer wants.

Sales force analysis

Of all the business skills that exist, few show the variation in performance existing between different salesmen. The best salesman commonly outperforms his average colleagues by three, four or even ten times; and the weakest can underperform by the same measure. It is not at all abnormal for only half of the sales force to account for in excess of 80% of the sales.

It is also exceedingly difficult to tell who is going to be a good or bad salesman without scrutinising their track records. Some studies carried out 20 years ago seem to indicate that good salesmen are those who act as problem solvers for the customer when he gets into difficulties. They are those who chase up on late deliveries, follow up on quality problems, and generally act as the customer's shop steward inside the factory. However, this behaviour is difficult to detect except by its effect on the sales pattern.

However, a detailed analysis of call rates, hit rates, and retention rates will indicate those salesmen who are not trying and those who simply are not capable of closing a sale. It will also identify salesmen who are very effective but have small areas or regions to cover. One must then decide which salesmen are beyond recall, which ones can carry bigger areas, and which ones are simply in need of retraining. At this stage consider the two types of training that are often effective: the 'how to close a sale' training and, often equally important, the training programmes that demonstrate the competitive advantages of our own products.

An analysis of the qualities of a good salesman is shown in Fig. 7.3, which reflects the results of a survey carried out by PA Management, on behalf of the Institute of Marketing. It reinforces the importance of the basics – in particular the preeminence of product knowledge and understanding customer needs. The list of attributes, in rank order shown, would act as a good checklist for drawing up a retraining programme for poorly performing salesmen.

A review of the organisation of the sales force's time frequently generates large dividends. Sometimes administration can be simplified to cut down the time the sales force spends in the office. Sometimes items can be called in where before they had to be written up. However, at other times it is possible simply to improve the way the salesmen organise their day. The most dramatic case of this that I have come across arose in a company targeting the various industries it saw as good prospects because of high volume use or because of their growth expectations. The salesman was on, let's say, Monday, going to all the chemical industry businesses in his area. The next day he was visiting the dairy products manufacturers; and the next day edible oil

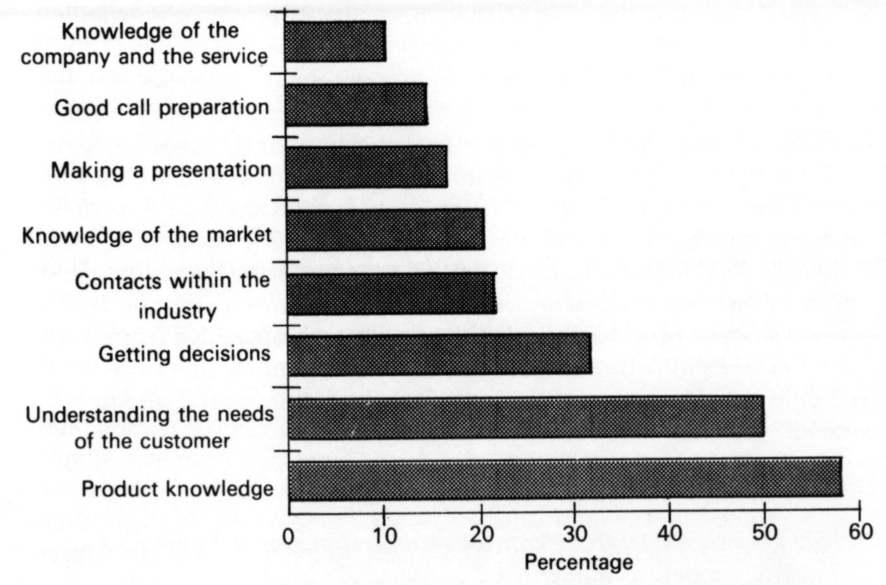

Fig. 7.3. Reasons for good selling performance: survey of 2,000 sales managers.

manufacturers. The result was that he spent a great deal of time travelling between plants and offices dispersed over his region. The solution for the whole sales force was to give them programmes based on the customers' addresses. This programme was designed to minimise their travelling time and added 60% to the number of calls they could make in a week, visiting exactly the same customers, but not by industry groups. New orders went up by 40%.

Often also the case is that the best salesmen are the worst organisers. They may allocate their time in an inefficient manner, and they may devote their skills to the least worthwhile customers. The company interest is in maximising the profit (or contribution) per salesman. Therefore, logically, the salesmen should concentrate their time on accounts that are most profitable, most likely to be won, *or* most at risk.

For simplicity's sake, classify customers into A, B, and C thus:

A – may account for 65% of profit and/or contribution
B – may account for 20%
C – may account for 15%

The likelihood is that A will contain very few accounts, which justify disproportionate activity. The rule for time allocation to these customers is 'whatever it takes'. The rest are allocated time more rationally.

One area of critical importance to sales forces is the incentive programme. It is extremely important that this incentive programme be tailored to create the sort of sales force behaviour that the management wants. Very often volume-only incentive programmes, based on the size of revenue the salesman brings in, in conjunction with excessive pricing freedom for the salesman, are the cause of unnecessary price wars. Preferable to these are incentive schemes based upon the gross profit earned by the salesman, measured both in his new sales and in the repeat sales he obtains. Generally new sales generate a high bonus just to reflect the difficulty in making the sale. Once again, such an incentive scheme should account for a significant proportion of the salesman's income and generally should have no upper limit.

New control systems

There are essentially three control systems that are vital to almost any company, namely as follows:

1. Call report summaries or sales force control summaries.
2. The weekly sales report.
3. The analysis of contribution of profits by product, region and ideally customer.

The first of these systems gives an indication of the activity of the sales force and its relative succcess. Careful monitoring of some of the ratios can give early warnings of problems or outbreaks of competitor activity. The ratio of quotations made to contracts signed, or the percentage of contract cancellations, or the ratio of outstanding contracts to current deliveries are all good indicators in the proper context of the way the company's fortunes are going in the market place.

The weekly sales summary is really just a dip stick indicator of the overall company performance. It can, however, be made a little more sophisticated to measure the effectiveness of promotional programmes, price changes and other changes in marketing activity.

The third report, the profitability analysis, is normally generated approximately once a month and is key to the management of the activities of the company's marketing activity. It should always show both contribution and net profit after total cost. While the former is a useful management tool, the latter is the key target that the company must meet to ensure profitability over any length of time. All products ought in the long run to meet this requirement or be withdrawn.

These three sets of control systems together are critical to the success of the company and should never be ignored. The chief executive should look at them all at least in summary form and occasionally delve into them in detail.

Advertising and promotional programmes

Discover whether any effectiveness studies have been carried on the advertising and promotional programmes. If the answer is no, it is normally wise to cut back all the programmes and start such analyses immediately. Do not be taken in by the marketing department's or advertising agency's mystique. The effectiveness of marketing tools is difficult to measure, but not impossible. If such studies have already been carried out, then they are worthy of re-analysis, since failing companies often have managements that ignore hard data rather than change their prejudices.

Pricing

Although pricing has briefly been covered under product analysis, it is a sufficiently important subject to be considered further here. For increasing the price is without doubt the quickest way of improving the profitability of a company. However, this must be a well-judged increase. It must be preceded by the following questions:

1. Are we already witnessing a period of price decline?
2. Is the pricing decided by the marketing department?
3. Are we in the habit of looking at only the contribution of our products rather than the full cost profit?
4. Are our competitors showing some signs of being in difficulty too?
5. Is there limited spare capacity that can be used to take away our market? Or segments of our market?

Any one of these symptoms is a sign that we should at least consider the possibility of a price increase. We ought, however, to be careful in carrying it through. Then a judgement must be made in answer to the following questions:

1. On which products can we increase our prices? Are there any which are highly differentiated from others in the market place, which already have high margin, which have a low purchase frequency, which are a small proportion of expenditure for the customer, or

which for other reasons have few competitors? Is there historical evidence of price elasticity?
2. Is there a point at which our customers become price sensitive? If we have a quality image, quite likely the customer will be willing to pay something for it, but not necessarily a very large premium.
3. How will our competitors respond? Should we signal them by raising our list price first and our discount price later?
4. Do we want to target certain customers for price increases and protect others? If so, should we consider a discount structure that reflects this requirement?

In arriving at our pricing decision we must look carefully at our production capacity planning and the trade-offs it often involves. The simplest way of assessing the price–volume–profit relationship is through a modernised version of the old breakeven chart. In the past, using the original breakeven chart, managers had to make a number of simplifications to make the calculation task manageable. Average numbers were used for revenue, for variable costs and for fixed costs. Today with a computer, a decent cost accountant and some time with the plant managers and sales managers, a much better approximation can be made. To this end it is necessary to proceed thus:

1. Determine points at which the fixed costs change. Typically this will be when overtime is incurred or when a new shift is put on or when a second plant is required.
2. Assess the size of these changes.
3. Determine the change in variable cost with volume with, for example, different products, different plants, different batch sizes.
4. Determine the variation in net prices and, most importantly, product contribution.
5. Construct the chart to reflect the above, with the revenue line built upward from the most profitable products.

The revenue line should show a slight curve downwards from the classical straight line for most normal companies, and the cost line will be stepped and curved. This is shown in Fig. 7.4. As can be seen, there is more than one optimum output, and neither is at the capacity limit of the plant.

A more extreme situation afflicts most loss makers, particularly those with more than one production unit. Figure 7.5 shows a situation that often applies. If the best customers were supplied only by the best plant (or on plaintime working in a multi-shift situation), then the company

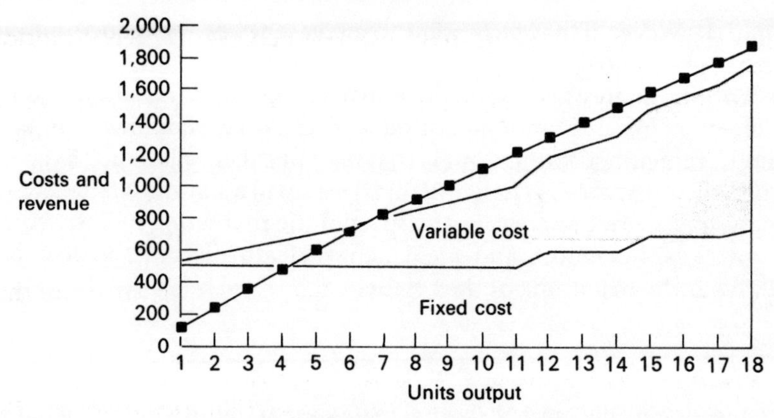

Fig. 7.4. Realistic breakeven chart.

would be profitable. Serving poorer customers, or providing poorer products, takes the company into loss. Cutting back on output would actually take the company into profit.

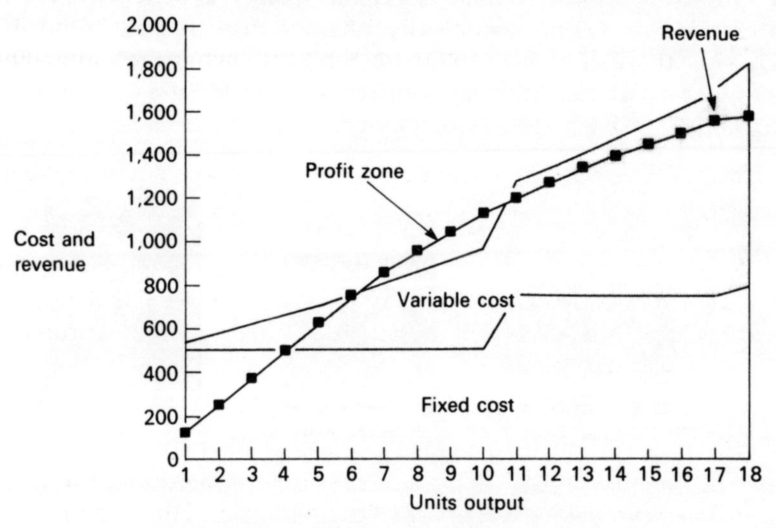

Fig. 7.5. Multi-plant or multi-shift breakeven chart.

There are two subtle permutations of this situation. Firstly, in some circumstances the graph in Fig. 7.5 does not show a profit at all; it may in fact show a minimum-loss position. This may well be the best point from which to start a cost reduction programme. Secondly, this is a static representation. It does not reflect competitive responses to cutting output. However, it may be possible to increase prices and reduce output to maximise returns.

All of this analysis is essentially a macroscopic approach to the joint problems of product rationalisation and capacity planning. The key point to remember throughout is that *none* of the numbers are fixed in stone. All are capable of change, if only by a small amount. Whatever we choose to do, price strategy is an aspect of the marketing mix the chief executive cannot ignore, and one which will feature large in his decision making at the beginning of the rescue.

Market shares

A stable, defensible market share is to be sought in the short to medium term. At the stage when growth is possible, the best routes are quality enhancement, product enhancement through features and additions, and product innovation, in that order. For a marginal company to initiate a price war is virtually *never* worthwhile; it almost never works, and it cuts the cash flow to ribbons. Product quality, as perceived by the customer, is a great enhancer of both profits and share. Indeed, as shown in Fig. 7.6, the higher the product quality, the higher the return on investment (ROI). Quality enhancement is applicable as a defensive as well as an offensive measure, remember.

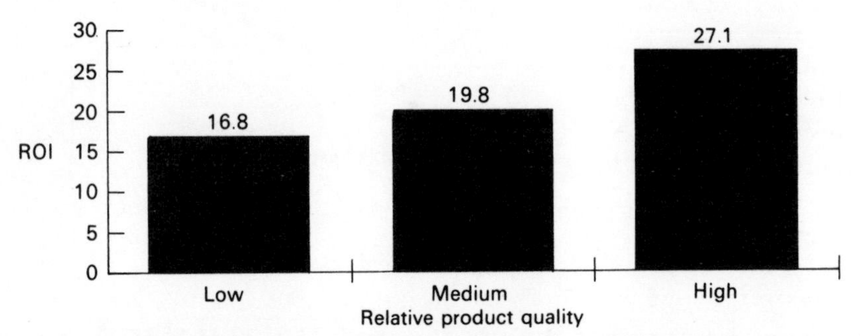

Source: PIMS database and Donald K. Clifford, Jr, and Richard E. Cavanagh, *The winning performance* (Bantam Books, 1985).

Fig. 7.6. Relative product quality and ROI.

INVESTMENT

Although Schendel and Patton show investment to be a significant part of successful recovery strategies and Stuart Slatter argues for acquisition as a route to growth, in my view additional investment needs to be viewed with great circumspection. There are several reasons for this caution:

1. Inevitably, cash flow is tight during company rescue attempts, and investment would obviously use up a significant proportion of it.
2. High investment levels tend to make companies behave as weak negotiators in their pricing.
3. Investment can divert management attention from the main problems, particularly if the investment is a diversification.
4. Being approached with ambitious investment programmes can undermine banker confidence.

Nevertheless, there are some circumstances under which investment is worthwhile:

1. When the company has been denied capital for a long time and is seriously handicapped by obsolete technology and a poor cost structure.
2. When *small* quantities of capital can give very marked gains (as when de-bottlenecking a plant).
3. When competitors are being sold cheap, and the investment-sales ratios can be *reduced* by acquisition. This strategy can be a *spectacular* winner in declining industries.

Even so, it is remarkable in conditions of capital rationing how much can be achieved to increase capacity, improve quality and reduce costs. Notably none of the above three-preferred capital strategies is necessarily inhibited by a rapid pay-back requirement in the early years of recovery (e.g. a three-year pay-back rule).

OVERALL STRATEGY

The overall strategy of the recovery program falls into two parts:

1. The rationalisation, or 'concentration on core activities', emphasis that marks the crisis, consolidation and control phase.
2. The development phase that is aimed at capitalising on success.

The former is a relatively predictable, analytical process that can work to a timetable. The latter is much more difficult to manage and impossible to quantify.

We start with the analysis initiated in the review of long-term viability in Chapter 3. The simplified version of Porter's diagram (Fig. 7.7)

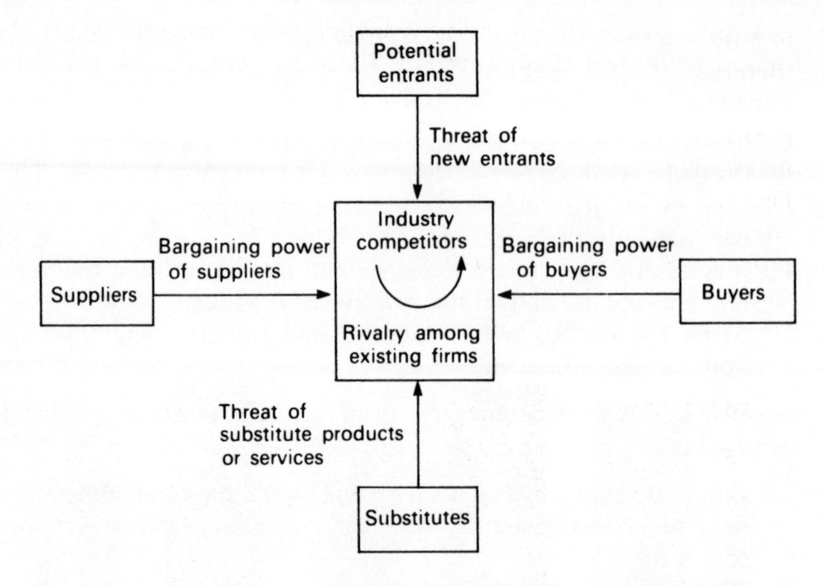

Sources: Michael E. Porter, *Competitive advantage* (The Free Press, 1985).

Fig. 7.7 The five competitive forces that determine industry profitability.

demonstrates the aspects of industry structure that have an impact on profitability. The aim is to seek out sectors of our business or businesses that minimise the pressures on profits and to divert our efforts in that direction. To do so we must decide upon the generic market strategy that best fits our strengths, namely one that fits best in Table 7.11.[34] That the company will fit into one of the 'focus' strategies is likely. The key issue is to find a sufficiently differentiated segment that allows an advantage to be developed. Indeed, sustainable advantage is all that matters.

One word of warning here about the issue of growth. Many managers are attracted by growth markets. Do not be fooled. Growth markets tend

Table 7.11. Three generic strategies

		Competitive advantage	
		Lower cost	Differentiation
Competitive scope	Broad target	1 Cost leadership	2 Differentiation
	Narrow	3a Cost focus	3b Differentiation focus

Source: Michael Porter *Competitive advantage.*

to attract more than their share of new entrants. Growth markets are therefore no more profitable than any other, as Fig. 7.8 demonstrates. Furthermore, growth is a cash-absorptive activity. Only when the company is financially stable, with a reasonable ROI (return on investment), will it be able to cope with growth of any significance (see Fig. 7.9 and 7.10). Timing is therefore important, as is the pace of change. That notwithstanding, at this point an understanding of the probable overall direction of the strategy will facilitate the transition to a stable, successful formula for operation.

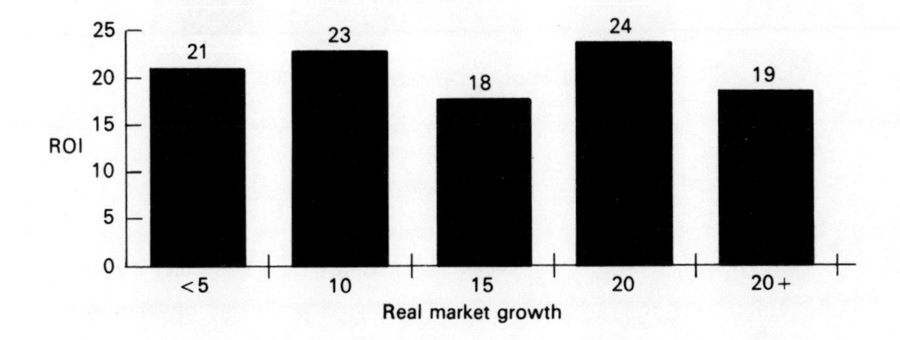

Fig. 7.8. Unimportance of growth to competent businesses.

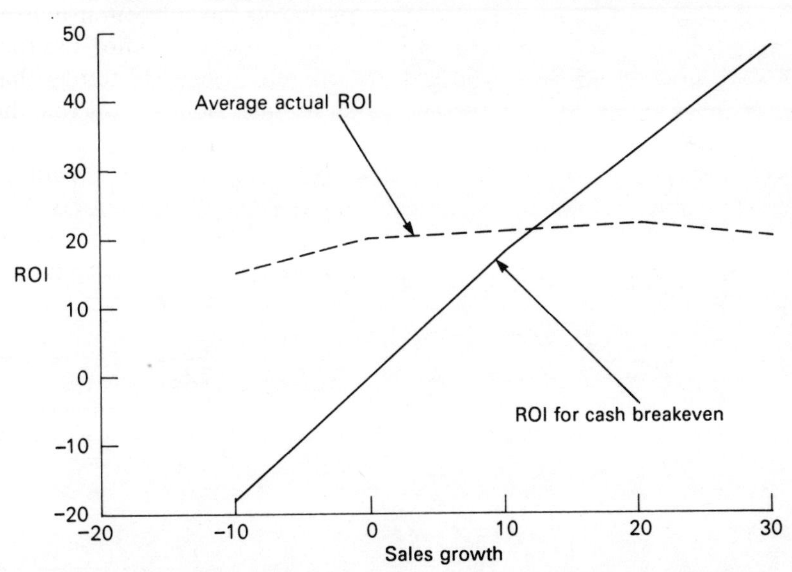

Fig. 7.9. Required ROI for breakeven cash flow versus sales growth.

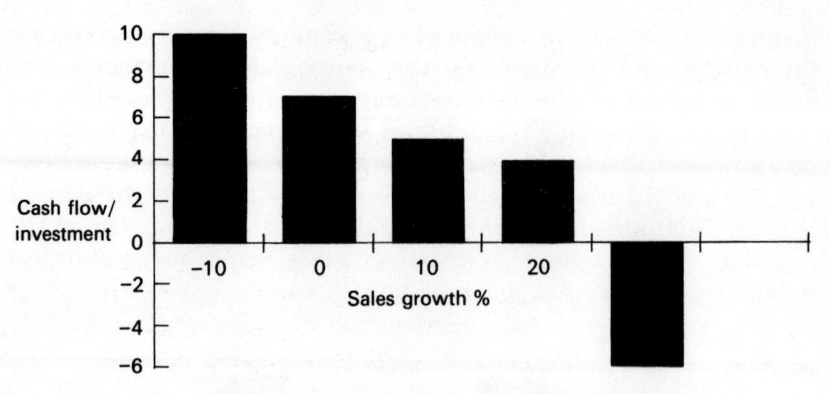

Fig. 7.10. Rapid growth and cash drain.

CHAPTER 8

The first hundred days

■

The first hundred days represents the honeymoon period in any rescue or turnaround. It is a time when the new organisation will be more responsive and will tolerate more demands than at any other time within the turnaround specialist's tenure. Accordingly, it has to be used fully to achieve the following aims:

1. Create room to manoeuvre.
2. Create climate for change.
3. Get control.
4. Initiate obvious strategies.
5. Gather information.
6. Test the team.
7. Organise the victory.

Each of these is a demanding objective in its own right. For that reason the first hundred days, as well as being critical to the success or failure of the whole exercise, will be the most demanding of the new chief executive. It would not be unusual in this period for him to work a hundred-hour week, namely all his waking hours.

Creating room to manoeuvre

The first aim is that of giving the organisation enough resources to survive beyond the first stages of rescue. It involves the refinancing of the company and the release of cash by asset disposal methods already covered in Chapter 7. Ideally, the refinancing is carried out before the rescue specialist arrives at the company and takes control, but it may have to be done in the first few days after.

The other aspect of creating room to manoeuvre is sharpening up the cash position. The cash position is a problem of very real immediacy, and so action to deal with it must be started on day one. The practicalities are dealt with in Chapter 7 but what must occur very quickly is a meeting with all the heads of departments to impress on them the seriousness of the cash situation and to request immediate action. In addition, some specific actions must be initiated, such as the following:

1. Stocktakes to determine what can be sold, what can be put on stop order, what we really need.
2. Action on overdue debtors, including creating an age analysis if one does not exist.
3. A limit on all non-vital purchases.
4. A daily review of the cash balance and bank position.

If a great deal of publicity or rumour has circulated about the state of the company, then there will be a need to se the major customers to make sure they are not considering taking their business to a more secure supplier. If there has been no publicity, then the chief executive will probably need to talk to the staff as a matter of urgency.

Creating the climate for change

The Schendell and Patton study showed that a company had a signficantly higher chance of recovering if it had suffered a proper crisis rather than fading away in gentle decline.[35] This observation holds the key to all company rescues, for it is the sense of crisis that precipitates the necessary management action within the company and creates in the workforce the willingness to accept very tough decisions, as well as the energy and drive and motivation to carry out those decisions. For this reason the rescue specialist has to do a great deal of perception shaping in his first days in office. He has to shake up the organisation and effectively bend it to his will, virtually immediately. He must inspire respect. At the same time he must not create a troop of 'yes men' around him, since he is unlikely to have the detailed industry experience needed to recover the company alone and will need to depend upon information and judgements from his subordinates.

Almost always there are very obvious, but unpleasant, tasks to be completed. These may involve the sacking of a senior manager or two; or more, a closure of an operating unit, the elimination of a department, or even possibly the prosecution of people for fraud or theft. The rescue specialist must carry out these tasks quickly and give some careful thought to the sequencing. For example, it helps the workforce tolerate the loss of jobs if they feel that the senior management who caused that loss are having to pay too. Therefore it is best to deal with the senior management before carrying out any severe employment cutbacks.

At this stage it is important not to lose any battles. If, for example, the new chief executive has to close some operating units and obtain manpower reductions in the ones that will remain open, he will be well advised to carry out at least some of the closures first. The trade union will then probably accept his willingness to take these tough decisions as proven and it will not be necessary to stand an unnecessary strike or have unnecessary closures as a part of the ritual dance of the negotiation process. Initial toughness, although apparently callous or brutal, can frequently minimise long-term harm to the interests of the employees of the organisation.

This approach – initial toughness – makes it clear that the organisation is in a serious situation and demonstrates the chief executive's willingness to make unpleasant decisions and take unpleasant actions. This is important to insiders and outsiders, to the employees and the lenders, creditors, customers and suppliers of the company. It will also, frankly, give more than a little anxiety to the people who work within the company, which at this stage is no bad thing, since the worst that a new leader can do is to leave employees with any mistaken sense of complacency about their future.

Giving a victory

Fear by itself, however, will achieve little. Frequently companies that are failing have also lost their confidence. The organisation and the people in it take an attitude that says 'we can't work any harder' or 'it can't be done' or 'everything has been tried' or 'whatever we do we are going to lose our jobs'. To change this attitude is extremely important, and so the chief executive should look to very quickly giving the organisation a victory. This can occasionally be difficult in the early stages.

As an illustration, one company that I worked in had a new plant which had been attempting to start up properly for nearly 18 months. For the last 6 months it had been operating at significantly less than half its designed output rate, and because of breakdowns it was in effect turning out only about a quarter of its total designed output. The workforce had given more than anybody normally had a right to expect. After 18 months of superhuman effort they were jaded and worn out. They simply did not believe that the problem was soluble, that this plant could be made to run at its full capacity. The principal reason for the plant's running below capacity was that it was poorly designed and that the operation had inadequate technical support and management to make it work properly. In addition, the technical support the company did have was distracted dealing with other problems in this particular factory. When it became apparent that the company could not have any chance of survival without correcting this output problem, I sent a questionnaire to the entire workforce to identify in their specific areas the problems that needed to be solved for their particular part of the plant to run at designed output level. It also asked them to make suggestions as to the least-cost way in which we could solve the problems.

A week after the questionnaire was circulated I had received one reply, and that was more of a joke than a sensible response. I then spoke to the entire workforce in teams and told them that if they wanted to participate in the future of the company, and indeed if they wanted to continue working in the company, they had better decide to put their minds to finding a solution to this problem. They had a chance to participate in the success of the company, but if they chose not to they had nobody to blame for its failure but themselves.

This pep talk led in the next week to a 98% response to the questionnaire. I then had to redirect the efforts of the technical staff entirely onto analysing the problems that had been identified, separating the poor advice from the good suggestions and drawing up a programme of amendments for the plant that could be carried out over one weekend. As soon as it became apparent that the improvement was technically possible, we instructed the marketing staff to sell all the planned output for the months after the beginning of May (the decided date of upgrade). We made quite sure that the detailed planning of such items as the availability of spares, the availability of technical support services and technical consultants (where needed) and, of course, the availability of the skilled manpower required was all properly done. Then on the Thursday before the critical weekend I found good reason to be in another country for four days. The upgrade was successful, and because I was not there myself, I could congratulate the entire staff of the company in achieving an unparalleled success on their own merits.

This is a rather high-risk example, but it characterises quite well the important components of a morale-boosting victory in the early days of the honeymoon period:

1. It was previously considered to be either very difficult or impossible.

2. It involved a very large number (in this case all) of the staff of the company.
3. It was important.
4. It was successful.
5. It was highly publicised around the company.

Thereafter, all the victories, major or minor, and indeed the names of the people that achieved them, were given great publicity on the company's newsheet. This confidence-building process is a key part of turning around companies with apathetic and demoralised management and staff.

Team involvement

It is crucial very quickly to rally all the teams in the company in enthusiastic support of the company rescue. That means their understanding the new value systems, the new strategies and the new tactics that the management will be using. It means setting up a communication system that will keep them up to date on developments. Much of the chapter on leadership covers precisely these issues, but suffice at this stage to mention one of the best and simplest techniques for doing this on a rigorous basis, that of team briefing.

Taking control

There are two aspects to taking control of a problem company, one is 'real' and one is psychological. They are both important, since neither is possible without the other.

PSYCHOLOGICAL CONTROL

The psychological aspect of taking control starts immediately the new leader arrives at the company. His demeanour in those first few minutes will send out messages that will ripple through the organisation for a long time thereafter. At this stage be assertive and decisive. Appear brisk and efficient. Do not tolerate poor performance even on day one. There will be people who feel this is a good moment to 'try out' a new boss. Any weakness now will be played on later. Therefore, if in doubt, aim for a firm rather than a weak hand even if it is shocking to the recipient. It is always possible to relax later; it is rarely possible to tighten up on a weak start.

CONTROL SYSTEMS

The second part of getting control is ensuring that the right control systems are in place. These control systems must cover the key areas of cost and revenue performance, and they must be frequent, quick and preferably simple. Table 7.1 in Chapter 7 shows frequencies that might be reasonable for an organisation. If anything, they should be more frequent for a company being rescued, when of course quite often the systems may not exist at all. However, some sort of system should be set up for cash, costs, sales and a few critical categories such as head count and capital expenditure. The others should be built as soon as possible. Furthermore, these systems should not just be used, they should be seen to be used. Questions that arise should be pressed until they are answered. Nothing focuses an organisation's attention on decision like the knowledge that the new boss is interested in it.

For example, once I introduced a variance-based, computer-generated daily report that revealed everything that had gone outside the limits of the process control unit of a factory that I ran. The report every hour simply lifted data out of the two computers that ran the factory, digested the information and produced graphical analyses of anything outside the limits. It provoked many questions. As I started to ask these questions of the senior managers, they started to ask them of their subordinates and the effect rippled all the way down to the operators. Suddenly the plant operators were paying a great deal more attention to the performance of their individual sections of the factory. All this from asking a few questions.

In practice there will be many other, more direct ways of demonstrating control in the first few weeks. Items of significant expenditure will require the chief executive's approval in the early days. Hiring, capital expenditure, wage increases, all discretionary expenditure, all will be subject to explicit approval. In addition, all large expenditures will be scrutinised as a matter of course. The result will be plenty of opportunities for challenging decisions and demonstrating the new values.

The operations diary mentioned in the leadership chapter, and with it the follow-up on decisions and agreed actions, is an important part of this information and control system. Apply it rigorously. Nothing should be allowed to overrun without a very good explanation, or without some penalty for the manager who has let it overrun. Even if the penalty is just a turbulent meeting with the chief executive, it must happen and be known to have happened. Finally, make clear that all operating decisions have to fit in with the new strategies being adopted by the senior management.

Profit analysis meetings

The focus of control activity is the profit analysis meeting. The new chief executive should steel himself for a difficult, not to say unpleasant, first few profit analysis meetings. In them he must put his stamp on the organisation: he must insist on standards of performance at every turn; he must be unforgiving about incompleted actions; he must be unwilling to accept missed targets; and he must be vigilant to ensure that he does not miss any weaknesses. At the same time he must exercise leadership in the truest sense: he must analyse, evaluate and advise. In a word, he must teach. And one of the lessons he must teach is that everything is evaluated by the profit and loss accounts, by the cash flow statement and by the balance sheet.

For example, with a product line rationalisation should come a number of predicted reductions in cost and increases in output of other products. When the product line is reduced, however, it should be monitored carefully. It is not unknown for the purchasing department to continue purchasing materials for products that are no longer being manufactured because people forget to tell them. When such a mistake has been caught once or twice, managers and workforce start to be very much sharper. Sharp correction such as this will be a persistent feature of the first few months. The systems are not just helping to make decisions. They are moulding behaviour.

Early strategies

The chief exective must initiate obvious strategies. Even the preliminary analysis will highlight some things that clearly can be put right at an early stage. For example, if costs increase suddenly and unnecessarily, they can be reduced. If a number of new product lines are unsuccessful, they can be closed down. And of course, in addition, one can take the most simple cost control action and increase prices where appropriate. The rule is that these moves are best if they are uncomfortable but not unsafe. Hence an extension of the time before a company car is replaced is ideal, so long as the maintenance on that car is not skimped. Putting off the repainting of the company's offices is also a good idea. Cutting back on overtime, and certainly a very rigorous look at expense accounts, is useful. These will not turn the company around; even added together they may not make more than 1% difference to the cost base, but they are very visible and they transmit a message. That message is that until the company is back on even keel, austerity is the order of the day.

Information gathering

The first few months in a new company is a time of voracious information absorption for the new leader. Whether it is control systems, technical reports, sales reports, complaint summaries, major supply contracts, purchase summaries, market research reports, trade press or even the personnel files, every possible piece of data will be studied. Those parts that are important will be systematised. In addition, enormous numbers of questions will be asked. Indeed, a vast proportion of those first months will be spent out and about in the company asking questions and discussing every aspect of the company's existence. Time will also be spent with customers discussing the product, competitors, our service levels, and their needs. Similarly, suppliers will be visited to gain ideas, commitments and knowledge about what they can do for us. Also worthwhile will be interviewing employees who have recently left or who are leaving, customers who have ceased buying from us and consultants and contractors who have ceased working for us. Sometimes these people give the most honest view of all. All this information will be compiled and analysed for the first serious plan within the first few months.

Testing the team

Within a short time the chief executive will have to assess the top two layers of management. Yet in the stressful atmosphere of the first few months it will be easy to make misjudgements about individuals. The fairest and most effective way to determine the competence of the managers concerned is by assessing their success at the tasks given to them. It is important, therefore, to ensure the following:

1. Everybody in the team has a number of things to achieve in the first few months.
2. The targets test the employee's principal mainstream abilities.
3. The tasks are measurable reasonably objectively.
4. They are monitored against agreed deadlines.

The aim is to assess skills, work rate, ability to interpret strategic directions into detailed actions and ability to complete those actions to a tight deadline.

Organising the victory

The most difficult action in the first hundred days is the organisation of the next stage. If he has not done so already the chief executive must take the following steps:

1. Draw up his business plan, itemising what *must* be done (e.g. become cash positive or start creditor repayment) and what *should* be done (e.g. make profit).
2. Determine what cash and people resources he needs. Most particularly he must identify the technical skills he will need (in its widest sense to include marketing and accountancy) and ensure that they will be filled. This will be difficult because recruitment normally takes time, but especially so when the company recruiting is in serious jeopardy. (This may well dictate the timetable for the whole rescue.)
3. Divide the plan into bite-sized chunks to ensure that the people he has are capable of succeeding in at least 75% of their targets, ideally much more in the early stages. Since much is to be done this will be very difficult; it is the reason for the division between 'must be done' and 'should be done'.
4. Identify the physical and organisational limits to the ability of the organisation to complete its task, and monitor them closely (e.g. maintenance systems, training inadequacies).
5. Identify the major risks that would end the game and plan to deal with them himself (e.g. strike, loss of major customer, bank withdrawal of support).

Much of this will, one hopes, have been done before the chief executive arrives at the company. However, some or all of it will have been modified as a result of information obtained since his arrival, most particularly judgements of people.

In summary, the first hundred days starts with a shock. it continues with a high level of energetic activity – what one US author described as 'hustle as strategy'. It leads to a sharp increase in expectations, matched by a lot of enabling activity; physical enabling, with stores, training, time and machinery; systems enabling, with information, speed and authority; and psychological enabling, with clear leadership, rewards, encouragement and a 'can-do' attitude. Speed is a part of the strategy, partly for the sake of rapid results and partly for simplicity. Speed renders things simple because it wrong-foots opposition and gives no time for reaction, be it by competitors or by the vested interests within the firm. Finally, the first hundred days is about learning, testing, evaluating and making the detailed plans and preparations for the major changes that the subsequent two years will witness.

CHAPTER 9

Consolidation and control

■

Whereas the emphasis in the first hundred days is on drastic action, both to stop the haemorrhage of cash and to shock the system out of the habits of decline, the theme of the consolidation and control phase of the recovery is *appropriate* action. This entire phase is one of transition. Early on it is the continuation of the increased discipline required to get the company into a survivable state. This phase still involves close control of cash, extreme cost consciousness, highly focused marketing and rigorous and relatively centralised control systems. The second half of the transitional period prepares the company for long-term success. The leadership style becomes more humane, controls become more decentralised, though with continued monitoring of a limited number of critical variables from the centre, operations become more quality conscious and marketing becomes more innovative. Over time as the financial structure becomes more stable and while asset management remains rigorous, it may become possible and appropriate to look at expansion through low-cost acquisitions.

Leadership

The principal concerns in the consolidation and control phase are the maintenance of the impetus of action and the sense of excitement and the creation and continuation of the pressure on the control systems to attain ever higher standards.

There often comes a slack period between one and two years after the start of the rescue attempt. This arises because the easy improvements have already been obtained and the control systems have been biting for a year, but the pressure to improve is becoming more and more difficult to satisfy. As fatigue takes its toll, impetus declines and the new system of management loses its novelty. The chief executive must be prepared for this, or the recovery will lose momentum and start to fail. In the words of Tom Peters, he must start to create a process of 'multiple Hawthorne effects' to keep the organisation's interest and commitment in these early days before it becomes self-financing.[36] Specifically, the chief executive must proceed as follows:

1. Ensure that ideas for action with long gestation periods are properly prepared, with proper information gathering, analysis, planning and any other type of preparation put into effect in the earlier period to enable action during this first lull.
2. Ensure that the vision of the company's future is properly communicated to everyone in the company in order to precipitate new thinking.
3. Ensure that the company is organised to enable many experimental ideas to be tried and to encourage the initiation of these ideas.
4. Initiate a reorganisation, probably at some time around two years after the start of the rescue attempt.

By about one or two years after the start of the rescue attempt the evaluation of many of the personnel of the company should easily be complete, any gaps would be identified and there will have been time to evaluate new people to be recruited, if necessary.

Organisation

The main issues that apply to organisation are really very simple. Firstly, there should be an effective communication system throughout the company. This ensures that everybody knows the strategy and value system chosen; it enables a sense of urgency to be maintained and it ensures that everybody is aware of the progress in achieving the company's targets. In a company where everybody's job is at risk, such communication is both a practical and moral requirement.

Secondly, the company should adhere to a visible systematic and persistent meritocracy in its approach to problems and to staff. This means that solving a particular problem should not be seen as in the 'domain' of any specific department. This means that habitual encouragement of the 'best person for the job' is supported by a regular reward system as discussed in the chapter on leadership, a reward system that gives everybody financial incentives for their performance, but also gives more power, authority and scope for action to those who prove themselves capable of solving the company's problems.

Finally, the organisation should include effective systems for action.

Most important in this is the habit of follow-up. Time and time again it should be hammered home that any job to be done will be checked upon. In addition, the company should eliminate many of the barriers to progress in companies. These barriers recognisable to any chief executive coming into a problem company, include departmental barriers, 'not invented here' attitudes and poor support (such as poor maintenance stores operations, poor information systems and inadequate training). The organisation for action also includes the encouragement of a trial-and-error approach to many problems. Finally, of course, it also includes the proper use of various control systems, as described next.

Control systems

Again, the most significant aspect about control systems is that built into them should be an emphasis on action. Many books that purport to describe control systems are actually describing information systems. A system can be called a control system only when it incorporates components that ensure that decisions are taken and implemented. A few years ago a US business magazine carried out a survey of the normal response to orders given by senior executives and discovered that only 50% of orders were actually carried out. The aim in a company rescue should be 100%, though realistically 90% is probably the maximum. In the first instance this means that the information system must identify deviations from plan (by variance analysis and other such techniques), determine their source and describe them in real rather than financial terms. This then makes it easy to answer the question that is posed by any information system, namely 'how can we correct it?'.

Another component of control systems is the obvious one of the systematic and inexorable habit of joint review of performance. Every director, every manager and every supervisor should be in the habit of regularly and frequently reviewing performance and requesting improvements from subordinates. Finally, control systems should involve a follow-up program like that described in Chapter 5.

Control systems of this type are less about intellect than about discipline. However, they are fundamental to the correction of the company's problems. Once they have been installed and run smoothly, it is possible to incorporate into them other important sources of information, such as competitive data, customer data and all the qualitative information that floods into a company in a changing market.

Also, once the controls are in place, it is possible for the company to apply 'bootstrap techniques' to improve its position. What this involves in essence is identifying good performance and multiplying it across all departments. The normal problem is that good performance is just as difficult to identify as bad performance, partly because most systems deal in averages. Control systems ideally should be designed not just to give the average performance but also (albeit on a less frequent basis) to identify the best and worst performance. Again, today computer technology makes this easier to do than was possible 10 or 20 years ago, and it is certainly a cost-effective use of information. The following example illustrates how the 'bootstrap technique' works:

> The sales analyst of a pharmaceutical manufacturer noticed that one division was doing slightly better than the other divisions in reaching sales quotas for a new product. The difference was hardly worth investigating, but it did catch his eye and he had some spare time that day. So he decided to break the division figures down into smaller regions, and found that one region was doing considerably better than the other regions in that division. And then when he called up the figures for individual salesmen in the region, he discovered that one saleman was doing tremendously better than the other salesmen in that region – enough to produce the slight edge the whole division was showing.
>
> It turned out that this particular salesman had deliberately disregarded the presentation provided by the company for introducing the product to doctors, and devised a selling approach of his own. Needless to say his approach was studied and introduced to the whole sales force – and national sales of the new product surged dramatically.[37]

It is remarkable how many times this occurs, particularly in an organisation that was previously sloppy. It is also the case that the good performers, once studied carefully, can in fact be improved further before their methods are generalised to the whole plant or to all the other members of the sales force or to whichever department they apply.

The other principal issue in this phase with control systems is the judgemental one of how to cope with the gradual transition from the sharp recentralisation that follows the emergency to the gradual decentralisation that is the hallmark of long-term successful companies. (Statistically, the evidence indicates strongly that a move towards decentralisation is an important part of successful turnarounds. There is, however, one exception to this, and that is circumstances in which a company determines that it will pursue a cost-minimising strategy. Study of PIMS data shows a quite clear advantage to a highly centralised organisation when minimum cost operation is the principal strategy.[38]

Very few companies can actually pursue this line of approach, certainly in Western economies today. Therefore, the move to decentralisation is the more general strategy. If you are pursuing a cost-minimising company, however, bear this in mind.)

The chief executive must make two essential judgements, one qualitative and one about timing. The qualitative judgement is exactly how to decentralise. It is about how to achieve delegation without abdication. This is done by identifying the one or two variables that describe the overall performance of the individual. Thus for a chief executive it would probably be return on investment. Anybody wanting to control a subsidiary chief executive should in the end tend to do so by one or two measures such as return on investment and, say, cash flow without trying to intervene in every operational control that he uses. For a supervisor of a production line, the measure would be volume of output that is up to specification and cost. For a salesman, the measure is probably the gross margin earned from his region or territory. These variables should *not* be relaxed. The information system providing these should continue to be controlled centrally. The methods of achieving the performance, however, should be left to the individuals, who are generally in a much better position than anybody else to make judgements about their own part of the business. This decision has implications for both performance and for morale, and of course as usual they are linked.

The judgement on timing is simple enough. Such decentralisation should start when the chief executive is convinced that his subordinates understand what is required of them, in knowing both what is wanted and how to achieve it. As soon as this understanding has been adequately demonstrated over, say, a three-month or six-month period, he should seek to reduce to the absolute minimum the number of controls that apply. If he selects the right controls, he will know soon enough if he has made a mistake. In that case he will simply have to reinstate that which he had relaxed. Since the information will still be going to the subordinate manager, reinstatement will not be difficult. It will simply be a matter of having an extra meeting and wider circulation on the report. *Minimum* effective control systems are economical in senior management time, effective in control and supportive of high morale.

Marketing

In the consolidation and control phase the worst loss-making products will already have been rationalised out and on a rough-and-ready basis pricing levels will have been corrected. Since marketing is the least scientific and most judgemental area of business, undoubtedly some mistakes will have occurred, and these will need correction. However, this apart, the marketing effort will fall naturally into two categories:

1. The pursuit of the main strategy, which will be to get the most effective sales performance out of the current product lines.
2. The search for new directions in the form of product improvements, new products and new methods of marketing the products to improve the volumes and prices achieved.

MAIN STRATEGY

The pursuit of the main strategy will dominate, and it will be a very controlled process. At this time the chief executive and the marketing director should have available to them margin reports on all the current products by territory, salesman, customer type and any other relevant breakdown. In addition, a lot of information should be coming in from call reports and daily sales monitoring. Along with the ancillary data, such as advertising expenditure, promotional expenditure, pricing information, and complaints and quality data, the implementation of the marketing strategy should at one level be at least a fairly clinical exercise. There is little or no mystique about this aspect of the business. At least if there is it should be dissipated, and quickly.

The aims should be straightforward. Although at this stage the long-term marketing and production strategy may not have been decided, any decision will be one of cost leadership (highly improbable); product differentiation (possible); or focused marketing, either with cost or product focus (probable). The difference between the first two and the last is that the first two are broad-target strategies, whereas the last is a narrow-target strategy. Unless the company is fixed into a broad strategy by its history, costs and capacity, it will probably find the focused strategy the easiest to pursue *at this stage*. Accordingly, the aims will be to proceed as follows:

1. Focus most of the effort onto the highest contribution and/or net margin products.
2. Re-establish quality, service and product advantage reputation.
3. Change the product mix gradually towards the higher margin sector without destabilising the competitive balance while retaining currently profitable volumes.

4. Establish and implement sales appropriate to the most profitable level of capacity.
5. Minimise market expense, particularly discretionary expenditures while attempting to maximise effectiveness.

For example, it may well be that the sales force has to be reduced at this stage. Manage the reduction carefully so that only the low performers leave. Careful management is the tone of all the actions here.

Nevertheless, at this level of experience there will be undoubtedly an element of trial and error in the process. It is therefore important to set up new tactical forays in such a way that their results can be measured. In addition, it is important to encourage trial exercises of new ideas, although to design them so that they do not jeopardise high importance accounts.

Similarly, the chief executive should maintain an 'eyes open' approach to marketing during this period, for example:

1. Monitoring what the competition is doing while the recovery is being attempted; (it may well try to steal a march on us at this time).
2. Looking at the extreme good and bad performances, as described above, for ideas, for best practice and to get an early warning of adverse movements in the market place.
3. Studying in detail the performance of the best salesman, the best product and the best customers and to help the process of discovering our strengths and improving our techniques.

NEW DIRECTIONS

The second aspect of the principal marketing effort is the search for new directions. Management literature is full of ideas about improving the ability of organisations to innovate. Most of the ideas are not very effective. Apart from the experimentalist approach already discussed here and elsewhere in this book, the other systematic approach to product innovation and product improvement that seems to work is that of customer involvement, and to a lesser extent supplier involvement, in the product design process. The customer has the overwhelming advantage of being most likely to know exactly what he wants, and also the advantage of knowing which of the competitors fits his bill best and when the competitors have been more or less successful in meeting his requirements. Customer-led marketing, in the sense of deliberately seeking from the customer ideas as to how to improve and enhance the product line base, is a systematic method of innovation that does appear to work.

Here is the chief executive of a medium-sized electronics firm describing a similar process:

> Our latest product was designed by development engineers, salesmen, service engineers and customers, not by me. We asked the sales people to crystallize all their recommendations. Then when we had finished designing we had a week-end conference and unveiled the new machine. I was able to say to them: 'You thought we were not listening. But this is your machine.' It meant that a salesman could say to a customer: 'I was responsible for having that built into the machine', and he could explain to the customer why he couldn't have in a £5,000 machine the £50,000 facilities. The following week-end we had a similar conference for the service men.[39]

Suppliers have, like the customer, an interest in our success; they also know what is more or less expensive for them to produce and probably are familiar with our own manufacturing process. Supplier involvement is an area that many industries have found successful as a source of innovation and accordingly they have copied the Japanese techniques of involving the supplier. The aim of this whole approach is to create a marketing strategy that increases market share, is very low cost, and is difficult to imitate or respond to.

In searching for new directions, the rescue specialist is using the sense of crisis, his own leadership abilities and the enthusiasm of his people to make up for the lack of resources. To get the flavour of how this approach works, read *The soul of a new machine* by Tracy Kidder.[40] It describes how one man drove his team, in a deliberately under-resourced second-division research and development establishment at Data General, to beat the highly funded first-division establishment and capture the market with the design of a new machine.

Product enhancement, minor (or at least low-cost) product innovation and major quality and service enhancement are all difficult to achieve. That is precisely why they are good competitive weapons; by the time the opposition has responded, the company's reputation is already established and one hopes the company is on to something else. Price warfare, in contrast, allows the competitor to respond rapidly; thus it permits no long-term advantage or gain in reputation and the winner is generally the company with the lowest cost and largest cash balance – not, usually, companies teetering on the brink of financial collapse.

Discussion of this aspect must end with a warning, however. This exercise, although inevitably free-form, must be limited in scope; and that means that senior management must be disciplined in its approach. Plenty of companies go under as a result of new-product proliferation. New products are cash hungry, absorb lots of management time and take a while to deliver profits. Cash, management and time are all in short supply in failing companies, and so this process starts late in the consolidation and control phase and it must be rationed.

Properly managed, this is a bridge on the route to success; improperly managed, it can lead to collapse.

Manufacturing and operations

A consolidation and control phase in manufacturing and operations hinges on aggressive use of control systems once again to force down through the organisation the importance of the 'least in, most out' approach to management. This systematic pressure for improvement should be on at least three levels: it should aim to give the best possible quality on a 'right first time' basis; it should aim to maximise capacity; and it should aim to minimise costs. If the first two objectives are achieved, we will already be on the way to achieving much of the third one. After the initial learning phase there should in fact be a significant number of new ideas shaken out of the system between 3 and 18 months after the rescue attempt has been initiated. If this does not happen, then one of the systems is not working or the company does not have a manufacturing problem!

The organisation for this stage is eclectic. Suggestion schemes, workforce involvement, incentive schemes, task forces and individual projects should all be committed to the pursuit of greater efficiency. The projects to attack will differ depending on the company, but they might include the following:

1. Capacity enhancement/de-bottlenecking, particularly if the plant is already operating flat out and there exists no low capacity-strategic solution to the company's problems. This is often surprising in its low-cost, high-impact results.
2. Materials control/waste reduction: a number of techniques apply, from value analysis to simple common sense and open eyes. This generally gives a significant but not spectacular gain.
3. Energy cost reduction: often a combination of minor modification (such as insulation), better operating techniques and good house-keeping can yield significant results. Government often helps with this.
4. Inventory reduction: everything from economic order quantities to just-in-time production is possible; stay with the simple solutions at this stage.

5. Labour productivity: a potentially enormous area; also a difficult one. This is best done by a *small* project team. There are many techniques – activity sampling, work study and work measurement, to name a few – but implementation is the difficult part.
6. Transport costs: often rapid results can be obtained by obtaining outside quotations, particularly if transport is an in-house operation. The same considerations apply as for labour productivity.
7. Make versus buy, and contracting out: often a rapid method of cost reduction, the external quotation should be the standard benchmark for internal costs.

This is not an exhaustive list. The best way to create such a list is with the ranked list of cost categories.

Financing

The financing phase should see the company making a gradual transition to appropriate funding mechanisms. Once all the interest holidays, acts of debt forgiveness and restructuring of capital have occurred in the crisis phase, probably there remains little scope for renegotiation. This is the phase in which management must meet the promises that were the quid pro quo for allowing the company to continue its financial life. Assuming, however, some serious progress in liquidating unnecessary assets and improving cash flow, it should be possible to structure the funding mechanisms such that the following occur:

1. Long-term debt corresponds broadly to long-term assets, and short-term debt to short-term assets.
2. The repayments schedule is manageable within the company's foreseeable cash flow.
3. The interest rate is reduced as the risk profiles of the company decline.
4. There is, in general, increased liquidity on the company's balance sheet to buffer it against any difficulties in the coming sensitive two years.

Assets

The pressure on assets and asset utilisation should continue in this phase. In particular, the discipline and control systems applying to working capital should continue to yield results as a result of the continuation of pressure and as a result of the learning by all levels of company management. This is the period in which we would witness the orderly sales of under-used assets and financially underperforming assets.

This may also be a time that witnesses some investment. Generally one should not encourage investment in companies that are already in a parlous state unless there exist projects that show a pay-back of not more than two or three years and preferably one year. However, occasionally companies get into financial difficulties because they are initially undercapitalised and have not invested at the same time or rate as their competitors. Under these circumstances investment may have to be considered, but it should be kept to an absolute minimum.

The exception to this rule has already been mentioned: it occurs if the company is in an industry that is generally in trouble. Quite often in these circumstances many cheap assets are to be had as other companies go bankrupt. If the company has sufficient financial support, then it may be possible to develop an enormous competitive advantage by cheap acquisition of other companies or parts of other companies. This acquisition may include whole going-concern companies or factories or inventories or even just spare machines. Some of these part purchases also have the side effect of ensuring the competitors *stay out* of business once they have gone out of business!

Just such a strategy was followed by Tate & Lyle in North America in buying beet sugar factories in the Midwest. With the minimum of capital expenditure they created a highly competitive and viable beet operation from the pieces of two companies. Similar strategies have been pursued from time to time by companies such as Hanson, Hillsdown and BTR.

CHAPTER 10

Capitalising on success

■

In a race, the person who comes from behind frequently wins. The same is true of rescued companies. If it is possible to maintain the momentum of success, then they can become top-class performers in their own market. The crisis-led kick-start into action that enabled the recovery can become a motor of progress to create the company's long-term success. This can happen because the necessities of rescue are very often characteristics of success. The key is to recognise which of these management practices are the common denominators and which ones have to undergo transformation in taking a company from the rescue phase to the long-term growth phase.

Leadership

Most modern writers on successful companies draw attention to the almost evangelical nature of the leadership exercised by the heads of those companies. They draw attention to how successful these leaders are in imbuing the organisation with their own personal values and thereby drawing from the organisation a behaviour that gives it its success in the market place.

Leaders bent on company rescue normally attack the problem with ferocious energy. They put in a massive commitment of time, in the early stages as much as a hundred hours a week. They make fiercely difficult decisions, generally within the public gaze. Accordingly, they inspire a range of intense emotions, ranging from fear to loyalty, from timid withdrawal to enormous commitment.

The trick therefore is to manage the transition from ferocious energy to one of passionate commitment, from fear to fun. This is not as difficult as it sounds. One reason is that in the first 18 months the leader will effectively have selected his followers. He will have determined who were successful and promoted them, and he will have removed the problem managers, those whose inaction or bad decisions were holding the company back. Thus at the end of two years the team will consist of people who have had victories, who feel they have been rewarded for a job well done, and who get much of their motivation from achieving a performance that was never previously countenanced. In such a team high morale is not difficult to achieve. And high morale and high performance together are a winning combination.

The previous chapter described the loss of momentum that can hit a company in its recovery period and the 'multiple Hawthorne effect' strategy of dealing with it. This strategy of continually maintaining a bank of ideas requires the chief executive and his senior staff all the time to keep an eye on the long term. It is enjoyable and easy to champion the project that delivers immediate results. It is a much more disciplined procedure to keep supporting the one that may deliver in 18 months' or two years' time. Yet the aim of the chief executive throughout the rescue must always be to create a company that is capable of being an outstanding success in the long run. These long-run projects are the vehicle to that end.

Strategy

If there is an overwhelming strategic message that comes out of recovery situations, it is the requirement to focus on necessities. No matter which section of the business or which department of the company we are talking about, 'back to basics' is an often repeated slogan. In a rescue attempt financial basics obviously come first, closely followed by operational considerations in their widest sense. The lesson to be learned from this is not to pursue diversifications, not to give in to the 'grass is greener' temptation.

This strategic single-mindedness is common both to company rescue situations and to successful companies generally. The implementation of the strategy at the tactical level does have some minor differences, however. Typically, in the early stages of rescue the tendency is to strip away and discard anything that does not pay its way. Peripheral product lines, low-performing sales offices, unprofitable factories, all are liable to be sold or rationalised in a rescue attempt in the pursuit of saving the main body of the company. In highly successful companies there is still this pressure, persistently maintained in the background; but it is also true that, for the very successful, strategic single-mindedness is accompanied by tactical open-mindedness. Such companies innovate systematically by encouraging a climate of experimentalism. New concepts are tried, new products are created and new processes are invented on a regular basis. The majority will not succeed, and the key characteristic of successful companies is that the failures are cut back quickly and innovations are brought forward to try. The willingness to spend money on many such loss-making attempts is an important part of a successful growth strategy. The key to its not becoming too high risk is the concomitant willingness to cut projects and generate new ones, all of which are individually small in relation to the company's assets and earnings base.

Tactics

In both rescue and growth situations implementation matters as much as strategy. For example, in Schendell and Patton's study of turnaround companies were two companies in the same industry using identical strategies. One of the companies failed miserably; the other was a great success.[41] Implementation of success is achieved by commitment to detail, commitment to action, and pace. Commitment to detail is more difficult in the turnaround because of a lack of time and, frequently, inadequate information systems. Nevertheless, such commitment is a vital component of managerial style. Commitment to action is critically important to both phases, and targeting and follow-up, the methods covered in the leadership chapter, are keys to company success for both rescue and growth situations. Pace, the sheer rate of achieving things, is actually easier in the rescue situation, where crisis and fear of failure act as strong spurs. Pace is more difficult to establish but equally necessary in a growth company.

Market responsiveness

The central skill of marketing in rescue companies and in very successful high-profit or high-growth companies is the ability to understand the customers' needs and perceptions of the product, combined with the ability to satisfy those needs in the best possible way at the least possible cost. This statement may be bland to the point of being anodyne, but it is the key to marketing success.

What it leads to at least in practical terms are value-for-money marketing, commitment to quality, and market positioning so as to allow profitable pricing.

The one serious change that occurs in emerging from the rescue stage to the growth phase is that some element of product line harvesting will be replaced by product line building. The cash imperatives of a failing company may in the early years force management into trading off market share for price increases. As the cash pressures ease, long-term profit becomes the fundamental aim and the share harvesting will be replaced by share-building and share-defensive strategies.

The long-term task

In managing the transition between survival and growth one must have a clear idea of what the final successful organisation will look like. The last decade or so has seen a number of empirical studies of success companies, the most successful of which have been *In search of excellence* by Peters and Waterman, *The business of winning* by Robert Heller and *The winning streak* by Walter Goldsmith and David Clutterbuck. From these studies emerge a number of common themes, which are reflected in the best research study in terms of its statistical foundation, namely *The winning performance*, a study of the most successful US medium-sized companies carried out by Donald Clifford and Richard Cavanagh.[42] Much of their study was based upon the PIMS database and involved establishing the impact of inevitably qualitative and even 'woolly' management behaviour on returns on investment (ROI). Clifford and Cavanagh identified a number of management traits that seem to be associated with success and then they identified how many were met by each of their sample companies. Figure 10.1 shows how stark is this impact on return on capital employed.

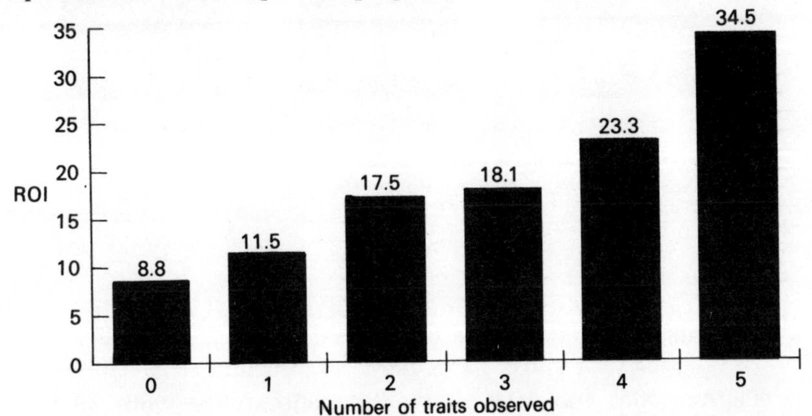

Source: Donald K. Clifford, Jr, and Richard E. Cavanagh, *The winning performance* (Bantam Books, 1985).

Fig. 10.1. Effect of strategic traits on ROI.

The management traits identified in the Clifford and Cavanagh research study are the following:

1. *Focus on how to compete, not where.* Essentially the study established what has previously been observed by Rumelt and others, namely that the industry the companies were in was less important than their method of competition within that industry. This is of course also the reason that companies such as Hanson, BTR and Hillsdown, who specialise in buying low-price non-glamorous companies, are so successful in achieving high returns on capital.
2. *Emphasis on innovation.* This covers conventional new products, improvement to old products, new ways of doing business, and finding new markets. Figure 10.2 shows the additional returns to be obtained from being a pioneer, an early follower or a late entrant. There is an advantage of almost 6% in being a pioneer – so long as you are successful. In the early years of a recovery being a pioneer is very difficult because of the cash demands and risk of innovation; when the recovery becomes established, however, the role of early follower at least, is obtainable.

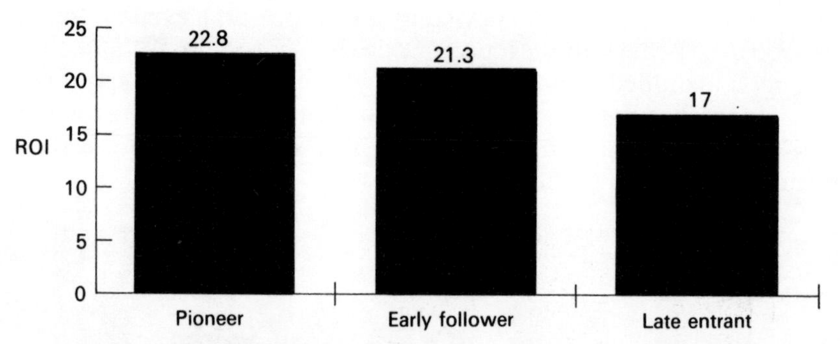

Source: The PIMS programme and Donald K. Clifford, Jr, and Richard E. Cavanagh, *The winning performance* (Bantam Books, 1985).

Fig. 10.2. Innovation.

3. *Skill at creating and serving niche markets.* It is easier to be dominant in a small market than a large market. This truism applies to all companies, but most particularly to medium-sized companies. Figures 10.3 and 10.4 show the relative profitability of small markets and large markets for medium-sized companies. They clearly demonstrate the enormous profitability of niche marketing. They also show the marked advantage gained from being first or

second in market share rank in such markets. Like innovation, finding and creating niche markets is in part skill and in part luck. It inevitably takes a number of attempts and reinforces the experimental or empiricist approach to success. It also favours highly customer-orientated marketing, since niche markets by definition have a smaller number of customers with specialised requirements that can be identified and met.

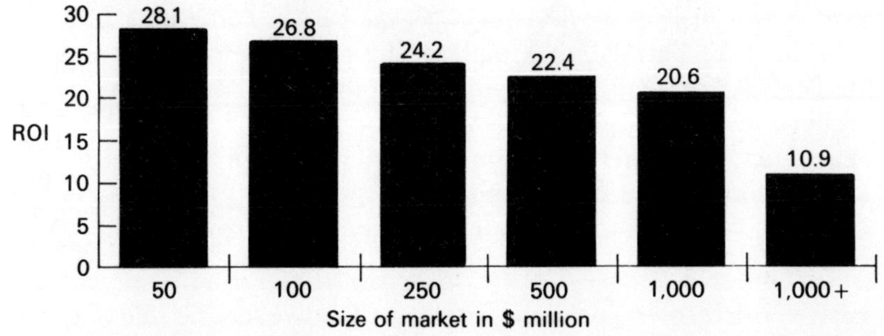

Source: Donald K. Clifford, Jr, and Richard E. Cavanagh, *The winning performance* (Bantam Books, 1985).

Fig. 10.3. Niche marketing: size of market and business performance.

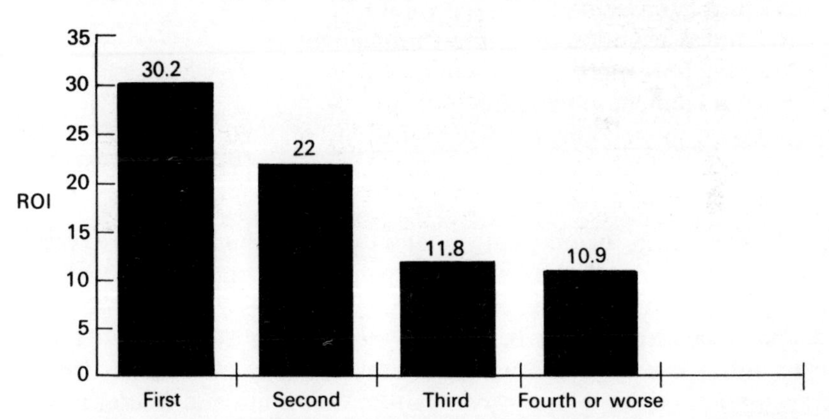

Source: Donald K. Clifford, Jr, and Richard E. Cavanagh, *The winning performance* (Bantam Books, 1985).

Fig. 10.4. Market share rank versus ROI.

4. *Ability to identify and build on strengths.* If a company can identify what is important to its customers, and who are its most and least successful competitors, it should be able to identify clearly its own

strengths and build upon them. This is something that companies often get wrong, usually by being too general about the strength (i.e. 'we are good at process manufacturing' rather than 'we are very good at sugar refining'). The key strengths are those that allow the company to meet the customers' needs most effectively at minimum cost. The more specific and the narrower the strengths, the more accurate the analysis is likely to be and the more useful the actions taken.

5. *Value as a more powerful selling tool than price.* For a long time it has been recognised that market share is a dominant strategic indicator of profitability. The reason for this is that market share is a reflection of the perceived value for money received by the customer. The better the value for money of the product, the more the customers that buy it, and hence the higher market share. In essence, value-for-money marketing generates growth and profitability.

How it is done

Clifford and Cavanagh identified six organisational traits of the winners in their analysis, namely the following;

1. A sense of mission and shared values.
2. Relentless attention to business fundamentals.
3. Treating bureaucracy as an enemy.
4. Encouragement of experimentation.
5. Thinking as customers and working hard on their behalf.
6. Counting on people and putting development and motivation at the top of priorities.

These may seem bland, but notably modern business observers generally agree on what makes a company highly successful. Indeed, Table 10.1 demonstrates the convergence of view between Clifford and Cavanagh, whose work is based on a detailed statistical study; Tom Peters (of *In search of excellence* fame), the majority of whose work is based on observation of many companies; Goldsmith and Clutterbuck, who wrote *The winning streak*; and Robert Heller, who wrote *The business of winning* after a long stint as the editor of *Management Today*. Each of these writers spent a great deal of time analysing and observing companies in Britain, the United States and other parts of the world. Their combined views, therefore, present a formidable collection of managerial wisdom, and it is in some way gratifying that there is such a massive degree of overlap.

Table 10.1. Formulae for success

	Tom Peters	Walter Goldsmith & David Clutterbuck	Donald Clifford & Richard Cavanagh	Robert Heller
Leadership and motivation				
Create sense of mission, shared values	X	X	X	X
Motivation high priority	X	X	X	X
Reduce levels of management, reduce bureaucracy	X	X	X	X
Incentives	X	X	X	X
Marketing				
Think like customer	X	X	X	–
Encourage experiments	X	–	X	–
Operations				
Concentrate on fundamentals (back to basics)	X	X	X	X
Financial	–	X	X	X
Operational	X	X	X	X
Reduce costs all the time	X		X	X
Encourage experiments	X	X	X	–
Systems				
Be fact/data orientated	X	X	–	X
Decentralise authority	X	X	X	X

Note: This is an assessment of common denominators; it is not intended to be, and is not, a comprehensive summary of the wisdom imparted by each of these authors. Any errors are, of course, my responsibility.

These organisational traits, then, are the characteristics that the previously failing company must persistently move towards. John Kotter described successful general managers as having a very wide range of time horizons, from one or two days to 5 to 20 years.[43] They must maintain at all times both a tactical preoccupation and a strategic vision. The type of company described by the studies referred to in this chapter represent the sort of long-term target that must always be the concern of the chief executive in a company rescue. When the company fits this description, when it is financially healthy and operationally successful, it is no longer a rescue case. It is then a winner. Thus these are the components of success we must aim for. They are the goalposts.

Endnotes

■

1. Stuart Slatter, *Corporate recovery* (Penguin, 1984).
2. Donald B. Bibeault, *Corporate turnaround* (McGraw Hill, 1982).
3. See, for example, J. P. Kotter, 'What effective general managers really do', *Harvard Business Review* (November-December 1982), p.160. See also Kotter's book on general management.
4. Gordon Donaldson and Jay W. Lorsch, *Decision making at the top* (Basic Books, 1983).
5. See Slatter, *Corporate recovery.*
6. R. T. Altman, 'Financial ratios, discriminant analysis, and the prediction of corporate bankruptcy', *Journal of Finance*, vol. 23, no. 4 (September 1968). See also Altman's book *Corporate bankruptcy in America* (Massachusetts, Heath Lexington, 1971).
7. R. J. Taffler and H. J. Tisshaw, *Accountancy*, vol. 88, no. 1003 (March 1977), pp.50-4.
8. J. Argenti, *Corporate collapse: the causes and symptoms* (McGraw Hill, 1976).
9. Altman, 'Financial ratios'.
10. Datastream, *Z-scores*, p.17.
11. Ibid, p.20.
12. W. H. Beaver, 'Financial ratios as predictors of failure', *Journal of Accounting Research*, vol. 5, (January 1967), pp.71-111.
13. Robert A. Comerford, 'Bankruptcy as a business strategy: a multivariate analysis of the financial characteristics of firms which have succeeded compared to those which have failed', University of Massachusetts, 1976.
14. PIMS (Profit Impact of Market Strategy) is a long-term detailed database that covers many hundreds of strategic business units over many years in many countries. It measures return on investment, cash flow and a large number of strategic determinants of these, allowing some general rules of business behaviour to be elucidated.
15. Michael E. Porter, *Competitive advantage : creating and sustaining superior performance* (The Free Press, 1985). Reprinted with the permission of The Free Press, a division of Macmillan Inc. Copyright Michael E. Porter 1985.
16. Ibid., pp.4-5.
17. Bibeault, *Corporate turnaround*, p.88.
18. Donald K. Clifford, Jr, and Richard E. Cavanagh, *The winning performance* (Bantam Books, 1985), p.154.
19. For the importance of implementation skills, see, for example, Dan E. Schendel and G. R. Patton, 'Corporate stagnation & turnaround', *Journal of Economics and Business*, vol. 28, (Spring/Summer 1976), pp.236-41.

20. Kotter, 'General managers'.
21. Ibid, pp.161-63.
22. Wickham Skinner, *Manufacturing: the formidable competitive weapon* (John Wiley, 1985).
23. For much of the content of Chapter 5 I am grateful to the Industrial Society for allowing me to use extracts from their material.
24. John Adair, *The action centred leader* (Industrial Society, 1988).
25. Frankly, I hate the term 'leadership style'. What this section really describes is a set of leadership actions that many people describe as leadership style.
26. See Adair, *The action centred leader.*
27. Woodruff Imberman, 'Who strikes – and why?' *Harvard Business Review*, no. 83610 (November-December 1983), p.4.
28. George Copeman, *The chief executive* (Leviathan House, 1971).
29. Chester Karrass, *Give and take* (Thomas Crowell, 1974).
30. Ibid., p.40-1.
31. See Schendel and Patton, 'Corporate stagnation and turnaround', *Journal of Economics and Business.*
32. David Davis, 'Computers and top management', *Sloan Management Review*, Massachusetts Institute of Technology vol 25, no.3 (Spring 1984), p.64.
33. See Imberman, 'Who strikes'.
34. To those unaware of Michael Porter's work I strongly recommend they read *Competitive strategy* (1980) and *Competitive Advantage* (The Free Press, 1985). Both books give clear insights to the whole question of competition and strategy.
35. See Schendel and Patton, 'Corporate stagnation'.
36. Tom Peters, *Thriving on chaos : Handbook for a management revolution* (Alfred A. Knopf, Inc.).
37. E. C. Bursk, *Advanced Management Report*, vol. 5, no. 7 (1984).
38. See note 14 for an explanation of the PIMS database.
39. Copeman, *The chief executive*, p.109.
40. Tracy Kidder, *The soul of a new machine* (Avon Books, 1981).
41. See Schendel and Patton, 'Corporate stagnation'.
42. See Clifford and Cavanagh, *The winning performance*, p.258.
43. Kotter, 'General managers', p.160.

Index